THE FIRST CHRISTIAN

THE FIRST CHRISTIAN

Universal Truth in the
Teachings of Jesus

Paul F. M. Zahl

William B. Eerdmans Publishing Company
Grand Rapids, Michigan / Cambridge, U.K.

© 2003 Wm. B. Eerdmans Publishing Co.
All rights reserved

Wm. B. Eerdmans Publishing Co.
255 Jefferson Ave. S.E., Grand Rapids, Michigan 49503 /
P.O. Box 163, Cambridge CB3 9PU U.K.

Printed in the United States of America

08 07 06 05 04 03   7 6 5 4 3 2

ISBN 0-8028-2110-3

www.eerdmans.com

This book is dedicated to
our three sons,
John, David, and Simeon

Contents

Preface

I have worked on the "historical Jesus" question since 1968, when John Howard Schütz took me as his student in the religion department at the University of North Carolina at Chapel Hill. A *B.A.* from Harvard College followed, in "Hellenism and Christian Origins," under the supervision of Zeph Stewart, George H. Williams, and Dieter Georgi. In 1973 James D. G. Dunn allowed me to be his first graduate student, at the University of Nottingham. My *M.Phil.*, which he supervised at Nottingham, was on the idea of atonement as preached by the historical Jesus.

Much later, in 1990, Jürgen Moltmann accepted me at the University of Tübingen as his last overseas doctoral student in systematic theology. The thesis I wrote under Professor Moltmann concerned the Pauline doctrine of justification as understood by Ernst Käsemann.[1] Käsemann himself allowed me to discuss the issues with him at length and in depth, especially the question of early Christianity's discontinuity and continuity with first-century Judaism.[2] He was worried that Paul's idea of justification, which he believed had originated in the

1. This thesis was published under the title *Die Rechtfertigungslehre Ernst Käsemanns* (Stuttgart: Calwer Verlag, 1996).

2. Our later correspondence is documented in "A Tribute to Ernst Käsemann and a Theological Testament," *Anglican Theological Review* 80, no. 3 (Summer 1998): 382-94.

ministry of Jesus, was being watered down within English-speaking theology. Peter Stuhlmacher, who also taught at Tübingen and who had long before been Professor Käsemann's assistant, made me one of his assistants during 1991 and 1992. I have given thirty-five years of my life to the study of the historical Jesus. This book is one result of that study.

I should note that this book does not fit neatly into either New Testament studies or systematic theology. These two disciplines are often separated in university faculties, and certainly in North America. This is not yet so in Germany, where I was taught to integrate the results of biblical research with systematic theological thinking. For that reason, this book is a monograph in neither of the two disciplines, but a study in both disciplines. My teacher, Professor Käsemann, could not separate that which in his mind and within his tradition were *one* study: the pursuit of theological truth in the context of biblical texts. This book is an exercise in New Testament theology.

A final important point to mention concerns the relationship of scholarship, specifically New Testament scholarship, to life. Does New Testament study relate to the experience of real human life?

Parallel to academic study, I have served in parish ministry for thirty years. For me, parish ministry and university research go hand in hand. They have become two parts of the same thing. Thus I affirm that the Christianness of Christianity — the historical-Jesus core — has got to connect with the experience of ministry. If the Christianness of Christianity does not connect with active ministry to Christians, then the ministry collapses like a house of cards. You cannot divorce the results of New Testament study from its effects on people — at least, not if you are in regular ministry. If you seek to be an integrated Christian, you cannot detach your head from your heart, the results of your study from your beliefs, your "pure" research from your empirical observation of real people, your hope to acquire knowledge from your hope to help sufferers.

You cannot separate your head from your heart. If you do, you will end up like the man who tried to serve God and mammon at the same time (Matthew 6:24; Luke 16:13). You will either feed your head and starve your heart, or swell your heart and wither your mind. We are all a unity, whether we acknowledge it or not. Biblical scholarship without the pastoral theme and motive serves no one. It is, in fact, sometimes the instrument for unacknowledged anger and retributive feelings toward the Christian church. I have observed this latter phenomenon many times, especially in university departments of religion.

I write as a convinced Christian. I am convinced, however, not simply by "the heart which has its reasons" (Pascal), nor simply by the evidence of Christ's discontinuous brilliance, which I take to be substantial and very real. I am convinced, rather, by the testimony of both forums: the text of the New Testament and the continuing daily catharsis that I take to be the essence of faith in a graceful God.

I wish to thank Nita Moorhead, who has worked with tireless dedication in the production of this book.

Thanks are also due to Simeon Zahl, who reviewed a draft from the vantage of his studies in German history and literature at Harvard University; and to Dr. Frank Thielman, Professor of New Testament at Beeson Divinity School, who, during a sabbatical semester, reviewed the manuscript for mistakes and gaps. Any remaining errors are solely mine.

Introduction

The Jewishness of Jesus Christ is a core theme in contemporary New Testament scholarship. His Jewishness is a main plank of contemporary Christian theology. Partly the response within Christian circles to the Holocaust, an emphasis on Jesus' Jewishness is now a given.

It is also the lens through which almost all other portraits of Christ from the past two thousand years are viewed. Many of the old portraits, and especially the portraits of Jesus conveyed through the theology of the Protestant Reformation, are now criticized for their blindness to Jesus' Jewish roots and origin, their neglect of the Jewish context for the religion of Jesus. Therefore, since 1945 an injustice in the scholarship, and within the Christian church as a whole, has been rectified. It is an injustice that was anti-Jewish in essence and anti-Semitic in implication.[1]

The restitutive re-Judaization of the historical Jesus, which is an overwhelmingly evident feature of post-1945 Christian interpretation of the New Testament, creates the impression that the *Christianness* of

---

1. Important statements of the idea that anti-Judaism and anti-Semitism are implied *in principle* in traditional Christianity are found in *Jews and Christians: Exploring the Past, Present, and Future,* ed. James H. Charlesworth (New York: Crossroad, 1990), and in all the books of Roy Eckardt. See also "Anti-Semitism and Anti-Judaism: The Modern Debate," in John Gager's *The Origins of Anti-Semitism* (New York and Oxford: Oxford University Press, 1983), pp. 11-34.

the founder of Christianity is elusive. Anchoring the historical Jesus in the thought world of Second Temple Judaism shapes a figure whose feet become set in concrete. The continuity of Jesus — in other words, the continuity of his teachings and life with first-century Judaism — can become so insisted on, so invested with decisive rather than secondary significance, that it becomes hard to make out Jesus' *dis*continuity.

When Jesus' thought is viewed primarily in Jewish terms, the traditional Christian begins to ask, What was all the fuss about? If this man were just the sensitive child and exponent of the religious milieu from which he emerged, then what was different about him in comparison, say, with teachers such as Hillel and Gamaliel? What was new or fresh about him? More to the point for the average Christian, what was new and fresh about Christianity? Is it a universal religion? Did it really make a break with Judaism? Or was it, deep down, the same thing? Was original Christianity simply a variant, for Gentiles, of Jewish ethical monotheism?

These are vital questions for all Christian theologians and also for the rank and file to whom their ideas invariably drip down. The uniqueness and the continuing universal significance of Christianity are at stake.

Throughout Christian history issues have arisen that are sufficiently important that they unsettle Christian self-understanding. In the fourth century of the Christian movement, there was the question of the nature of priesthood: the Donatist schism.[2] The church in North Africa split over this question. At the end of the nineteenth century, there was the burning question of whether the Old Testament should

---

2. The church in Carthage split over the consecration of Bishop Caecilian in 311. The Donatists believed his consecration was invalid because the bishop who consecrated him had recanted his faith during the persecution of Christians under the Emperor Diocletian. In other words, the Donatists tied the validity of Caecilian's being a bishop to the moral character of his consecrator. The orthodox party in the church argued that the consecration was objective finally, and that its validity did not depend on the weakness of the person. The Christian church split over this issue for exactly one hundred years.

be considered divine revelation or (inaccurate) human history: the Colenso case. The church in South Africa divided over the question.[3] Every century — every decade — of Christian existence has had a presenting issue of conflict and schism; absorbing, enervating conflict; wearisome, draining division.

The presenting issue for Christianity today is its relation to Judaism, and, more specifically, the relation of Jesus of Nazareth to the religion of Judaism. This issue is of ultimate and not penultimate importance. Like the question of Jesus' divine identity, which came to the fore in the second century of Christian existence, and like the question of the divine Unity in relation to the Son's separateness from the Father, which came to the fore in the third and fourth centuries, the question of the historical Jesus in relation to Judaism is of similar importance today.

What happened to give this question of the relation between Jesus and his Judaism such importance for Christians? It was the Holocaust. The Holocaust turned a brilliant, almost blinding light on the inherited views of most Christians and their churches concerning Jews and Judaism. That light threw the theological world of Christianity into a high relief of guilt, chaos, and retraction. This was partly because Christian theologians as a whole were silent in relation to the suffering of the Jewish people before and during the Holocaust. "One effect [of the Holocaust] was to make the Christian world see how wrong the relationship between Jew and Christian had been and to take a fresh look at it."[4]

The study of Jesus' life has, since the rise of Holocaust awareness, reflected a pervasive and deep-seated diffidence on the part of many Christians in relation to their Jewish heritage. The study of his life now bears the imprint of Holocaust guilt and Christian shame.

3. Bishop John William Colenso (1814-1883) of Natal in South Africa was a liberal critic of the Old Testament and of the book of Romans. He was deposed in 1863 but challenged his sentence. He was excommunicated in 1866. The diocese of Natal split over Colenso's status, which was related to his interpretation of the Bible. In 1911 the split ended, but its echoes continue today in South Africa.

4. James Atkinson, *Christianity and Judaism: New Understanding, New Relationship* (Oxford: Latimer House, 1984), p. 43.

The drive, therefore, to draw lines of continuity connecting Jesus to Judaism has become extremely strong. The breaks in such lines of continuity — the *dis*continuities, in other words — have become a little embarrassing, a little close to historic Christian anti-Judaism and thus all too close to anti-Semitism. This is why current Christian thinking about the historical Jesus stresses and underscores the continuity of his life and words with the Jewish background from which he came. The Christian world, discovering itself for reasons of Holocaust guilt to be on the defensive, has sought to re-Judaize its principal figure. Jesus of Nazareth has become enculturated in the ancient past.

Can such a heavily determined figure of history continue to exist as a universal person for the world? Can a Jesus who is solidly contextualized within the world of Second Temple Judaism also be the object of a worldwide religion?

In the question of Jesus' Jewish context, we are up against a perennial issue in the history of thought. What is the relation of a general concept or idea to the context from which or in which it originated? Nothing comes from nothing. Haydn wrote string quartets before Mozart wrote his. Sondheim wrote *West Side Story* before he wrote *Company*. Jesus taught in continuity with the context in which he had been reared. He was taught by the rabbis and in turn taught in their synagogues.

But a Jesus in unbroken continuity with Judaism is problematic for traditional Christianity. A Jesus in unbroken continuity with Judaism can give the impression that traditional Christian theology has been guilty of making him into a "Christ-figure," a savior-messiah very different from the man who really lived and really was. A Jesus primarily in continuity is hard to recognize as the one whom Christians worship as "my Lord and my God" (John 20:28).

There is an old distinction in theology between the "Jesus of history" and the "Christ of faith."[5] This distinction refers to the difference

5. This distinction goes back to the German theologian Martin Kähler (1835-1917), whose book *The So-Called Historical Jesus and the Historical Biblical Christ* (1988 English edition) split the two entities. Regarded at the time as a "conservative" work of New Testament interpretation, its effect has been to dehistoricize the christological Christ of history.

between the historical figure of Jesus in his actual life and death and the divine object of faith who became transnationally real to believers after the resurrection. The distinction is correct in the sense that we all know what a huge difference exists between an actual person we love who lived and died in the past and the place that person now holds in our heart and memory. We romanticize the one who died. Or maybe we curse him. We paper over the bitter memories in favor of the good ones, or forget the good memories and focus on the bad. We remember selectively, depending on our original attitude toward the person. Such selectivity would have also had to be true, in memory and recall, regarding Jesus who became known as Christ. Inevitably a gap would come to exist between the person as he was in life and the person who lived on in the mind's eye. That much is obvious and reasonable.

The problem comes when Christian theologians regard the gap between the Jesus of history and the Christ of faith as being deeper than it really is. The impression left on the mind and memory by someone's action or word is based on that action or word. There is projection, naturally, but the impression that lingers came about from an event that really took place. Every memory begins with something that occurred in time. The overwhelming impression created by Jesus on his hearers has to have been rooted in something that happened. Jesus' memory among the first Christians has to have been rooted in remembered things.

What has occurred within wide sectors of Christian self-understanding since 1945 has been so to detach the Jesus of history from the Christ of faith that it has become hard to say whether the Christ whom Christians worship is the same as the rabbi Jesus who taught and lived within a specific time and place. Jesus in almost total continuity with Second Temple Judaism comes to have a fragile and tenuous connection with the Christ whom Christians assert they know and love. When Christ's continuity with his original context is the main thing, Christianity starts indeed to become a variant of first-century Judaism. Christianity begins to become a biblical monotheism open to Gentiles but not different in substance from the broad norms of Jewish ethical teaching. Christianity begins to become a form of Judaism for non-Jews. The substance of this book is a refutation of that idea.

The idea that Christianity is Judaism for Gentiles is not a straw man. It has always been one possible option in the history of what Christ began. Even as Jesus left, there were three options for the development of Christianity. The first was to consider it a sect of Judaism that believed in him as the Messiah but regarded the Law of Moses, its commandments and precepts, as being still in effect *in toto*. The second option for the development of Christianity was to regard it as an opening up of the blessings of Judaism to Gentiles, according to which Gentiles could become Jews without having to be circumcised or live according to the Jewish diet. On this line, Christianity was Jewish monotheism without specific ethnic boundary markers. The third alternative was to understand Christianity as new in substance, involving a materially original approach to the Law. Most traditional Christians still believe, or think they believe, the third version.

The idea that Christianity is more or less Judaism for Gentiles is not an idea to be resisted simply because it flies in the face of most traditional Christian teaching. The idea that Christianity is more or less Judaism for Gentiles needs to be refuted because it is not true.

Jesus was discontinuous with Second Temple Judaism in vivid and memorable ways. He came with a *novum* — or, better, *novums*. From a traditional Christian's point of view, many of his teachings and actions appear like, sound like, feel like "Christian" teachings and actions. They read like words and works of mercy that most traditional Christians would regard as characteristically Christian. The significance of such words and works, played out in the theater of first-century Jewish sectarian debate and against the backdrop of an extremely sensitive and also threatening political situation, became centrifugal. What began as relatively small disturbances in conventional thinking became a Mount St. Helen's in the course of thought and intellectual reception. There is a connection between things Jesus said and taught and things that Christians understand to be classically Christian. Such "Christian" things include compassion in the face of merited penalty, inwardness as opposed to show, humility as opposed to the receiving of credit, self-denial as opposed to self-assertion, peacefulness as opposed to violence in any form, and so on. Whether such things really are uniquely or self-evidently

"Christian," as opposed to Buddhist or Stoic, Muslim or Jewish, remains to be weighed in my argument. But there is no doubt that most traditional Christians would regard such values as part of their way.

This book affirms the discontinuity of the historical Jesus in relation to his context. It decontextualizes Jesus in relation to the hypercontextualization of him in recent Christian theology. Specifically, it affirms the continuity of Jesus with the idea of grace-Christianity as over against Law-Christianity, as that antithesis was understood by the Protestant Reformers of the sixteenth century.

I believe Luther did well to grasp the discontinuity of Christ's teachings in his famous thorough distinction between the Law and the Gospel. The Reformer caught a fair glimpse of something important when he underscored the breakthrough of grace into world events that occurred at the coming of Christ. It is possible to regard familiar icons of a very Christian Jesus, such as Bertil Thorwaldsen's *Compassionate Christ*,[6] or Warner Sallman's *Head of Christ*,[7] and see in those conceptions an enduring continuity, in visual form, of core Christianness.

Jesus of Nazareth, the historical Jesus, was the first Christian. The phrase is actually controversial. It expresses a continuity between Jesus and Christianity with which much contemporary New Testament scholarship has become uncomfortable. It puts the man on a collision course with his past, a man "whose life, though blameless, had incurr'd perpetual strife."[8]

I will not be saying that Jesus was an unusual rabbi who became caught up in a political vise turned by the Romans. I will say, rather, that Jesus broke fundamentally with his past, as a maturing man might, at least for a period, with his father and mother or sisters and

---

6. The statue was created in 1821 for the Christiansborg Palace Church in Denmark. It was copied hundreds of times in plaster and marble and depicts Christ on earth in terms of a strong and tender welcome.

7. The picture was painted in 1924 and became famous when it was "discovered" in 1933 by an American seminary professor at McCormick Theological Seminary.

8. William Cowper, "Conversation," *Poetical Works* (London: Frederick Warner and Co., n.d.), p. 185.

brothers. I shall be saying that the birth of Christianity, and its parting of the ways in relation to Judaism — so awesome and also so tragic a phenomenon in world history — is implicit in the man himself. Christianity was not the creation of St. Paul, nor of St. Peter, nor of the Emperor Constantine, nor of St. Augustine.

Jesus of Nazareth was the first Christian.

The sensitivity of my book's theme weighs on me. The issue of Jesus and his central significance for Christians is at the heart of all interreligious dialogue within a world riven by religiously engendered divisions. September 11, 2001, will be with us for decades, and in a sense forever. Relations between Islam and Christianity have shipwrecked unendingly over the question of Christology, Christ's identity in comparison with the Prophet's. The identity or divine uniqueness of Jesus *separates* Christianity from Islam, for Islam reveres but does not worship its founder. Christology, which is the assertion of Jesus' specialness theologically understood, is the wall of partition between Christianity and other religions.

Christology is also the barrier, the impassable barrier, that exists between the daughter, Christianity, and the mother, Judaism. An attempt, like this book, to magnify the dissidence of Jesus in relation to the Judaism that birthed him is bound to enter some deep waters. Could it, in fact, trouble the waters? Could it thicken or prop up the "dividing wall of hostility" (Ephesians 2:14) between mother and daughter? One reason for the magnetic attraction of the Jewish Jesus in the contemporary milieu is the way in which this Jesus starts to *pull down* the old costly barrier between Christians and Jews. If Jesus was primarily a Jewish teacher and a sympathetic exponent of the Law of Moses, then his Christian followers have made a sorry mistake in building up their side of the partition against the religion of Judaism. Christianity's Christianness could be a mistake, a form of assertion and self-righteousness that led directly to the Nazi Holocaust. By foreshortening the distance between Jesus of Nazareth and the Judaism that nurtured him, we might be combating actively and constructively the virulent virus of anti-Semitism. It has been a particularly resistant virus. "Rabbi Jesus," the contextualized Jesus of our new age, could prove an influential resource in immunizing the world against a repeat of 1933-1945.

The charge against Christianity, that it created a climate in which the Holocaust became inevitable, is a principal issue in Christian identity today. Nothing is more damaging, nothing whatever is more vitiating to Christian self-confidence than the accusation of intrinsic, incipient anti-Judaism. That charge depletes and exhausts the Christian mission to its very core.

A Jesus contextualized, on the other hand, a Jesus whose existence in history is not universal but is rather essentially and centrally derivative, a Jesus anchored in Judaism and not in fundamental tension with it, such a Jesus fits the spirit of the age. In some respects he fits the needs of our age.

So why write this book? Does anyone do well to contend for a Jesus whose interpreted departures and remembered independence from Judaism are divisive by nature?

The answer, this author's apology, has got to lie in the strength of Jesus' unique message itself. The answer has to lie in its inherent substance. His message, its resonance and authority in relation to empirical human experience, has to be sufficient to override the deterrent of religious harmony for its own sake. There has to be something in the substance of the difference Christ imported that is worth the risk of division. I have to believe that the good of magnifying the discontinuity finally outperforms the good that is also involved in suppressing difference for the sake of unity. This is an uncomfortable possibility, for it carries the implication that truth may be superior to peace, or better, that truth may be necessary in order to create peace. Can a Christian really say that?

The resistance of my Christian conscience to speaking about Jesus' difficulties with his inherited religion, difficulties that may attend the dismantling of a newer religious equilibrium built on a religiously Jewish and therefore un-dissonant Jesus, can only be overcome by the hope that a new or better way to reconciliation follows from the assignment of difference. In other words, this book, which heightens rather than reduces the otherness of Christ, has to aspire to the very reconciliation it appears to threaten. This book, to be justified in a period of interreligious division, must finally play its part in building bridges.

James Atkinson, a Church of England evangelical with deep roots in the Reformation and also a sincere lifelong love for the Jewish people, says it well:

> A Christian believer with a high Christology and a deep experience of the living Christ may be charged with intolerance in that he tolerates no explanation of Christ other than that of the New Testament, for no other explanation makes sense either of the New Testament evidence or of his own experience. . . . When faith burns with the intensity of a Luther or a Calvin, of a Tertullian or a Chrysostom, that bright positive light may flicker with the negative streak of intolerance. Intolerance may degenerate into opposition in word or thought, and finally in deed. . . . We must ever uphold our original ideal and practice of speaking the truth in love. Many have failed to do so, even great and tolerant men like Erasmus. When we fail we must recall that Christianity is the art of making fresh beginnings and simply start all over again.[9]

A *Christian* Jesus has got at the end of the day to be good news for Judaism and for Jews. A non-Jewish Jesus has got to be good news for Judaism. Otherwise, such a Jesus should only be approached, as George Steiner wrote, with a long spoon.[10]

I could not look in the mirror if I thought that the discontinuities I discern in Jesus from thirty-five years of study are harbingers of reaction and violence. To impute an overriding universality to Christ's teachings beyond the particularities of every other religion and worldview can be justified in the current world climate of religiously

---

9. Atkinson, *Christianity and Judaism,* p. 50.

10. See his 1991 essay "Through That Glass Darkly," in *No Passion Spent: Essays 1978-1995* (New Haven and London: Yale University Press, 1996), pp. 328-47; and his 1995 "Two Suppers," same volume, p. 419.

rooted conflicts only if the hope is brought to bear that the very peace and human solidarity that religion seems destined to undermine can in fact be produced by religion. Deconstructing an exaggerated continuity between Judaism and Christianity can be justified only if it results in improving the fortunes of the family of humankind.

This book is a positive word. I believe that Jesus' distinctive contribution to thought builds up rather than tears down. His distinctive contribution to thought engenders human solidarity, finally, and dissolves ethnic and racial distinctions. It dissolves otherness. It opts for healing by means of acceptance, and it is explicitly free from the principles of power and force as means to ends. It binds together human beings as people of unexceptioned human paralysis — needing, with no single exception, the grace of God. This is the good news of original sin, the constructive content of the even distribution of human nature. The human problem that Jesus diagnosed forms a divisionless worldwide community of need. The God whom he envisioned as responsive to human need and also human projection is kind and benign.

I am content to emphasize the difference between Christ and his context in order to attend to the potential universality of his dissident, dissonant message. His discord with his origins made a garden without walls, a country without borders.

The aspiration of this book is not a particularly safe one. It could be open to the charge of reopening a wound on the site of a battle that ended badly, very badly, for Christianity. But there is a better hope that sanctions the effort. It is the hope of accruing to Christian believing a substantiated confidence in Christ's universal message about human nature and the relation of human nature to God the Judge. It is not a question of "seek the truth, no matter where it leads, no matter what it costs."[11] It is rather the question of whether any one person's words can carry meaning for "all sorts and conditions of men and women" *(Book*

---

11. The motto in its essence is often attributed to William Sparrow, who taught at the Virginia Seminary of the Episcopal Church from 1841. Sparrow, an Episcopal evangelical, pressed the young Phillips Brooks (1835-1893) to combine intellectual open-mindedness with a broadly evangelical Christology.

of Common Prayer). Jesus' uniqueness could consist in a universal description of the human problem that withers all distinction among people, including even those of gender, race, and power. The dissonant message of Christ could be fruitful for peace on earth rather than destructive of it. That is the hope of this book. That is what drives it.

In order to hear the notes of discontinuity within the teachings of the historical Jesus, we have to begin by reviewing the three so-called "quests for the historical Jesus." These "quests," undertaken over the past one hundred and fifty years, have been scholarly searches after the man as he really was.

The first quest ended in the early 1900s. Like Scott's expedition to Antarctica, the first quest ended in complete disaster. The second quest, in the 1950s and 1960s, made important progress. The results of the second quest have been forgotten, but have never been disproven.

The third quest, which began in the 1980s and continues today, involves two approaches or strands: first, the so-called Jesus Seminar, which understands Jesus primarily in Greco-Roman philosophical categories; and second, the Jewish Jesus of the post-Holocaust era. In both strands, the third quest counters the traditional Protestant or Protestant Reformation view of Jesus, with its antithesis of Gospel in opposition to Law. Chapter One weighs the three quests, the aspirations of each and also the failures of each, and asks whether a fourth quest, building on the second, might not now be possible.

Chapter Two looks at some of the evidence for Jesus the Jew. Specifically, this chapter looks at the rabbi Jesus of Nazareth. The late David Flusser's majestic *Jesus* (Jerusalem, 3rd ed., 2001) is a good place for traditional Christians to begin in order to build up the true colors of his Judaism, yet without painting them on in such a way as to fasten his mouth shut.

David Flusser's approach to the question of continuity, the unquestionable lines of continuity that tie Jesus' words to his Jewish context, is an ideal way for traditional Christians to approach the question of Jesus' Judaism, because Flusser came at the man from the Jewish side of the faith-divide, yet with an almost unparalleled admiration for what he found. Flusser was a religious Jew who admired Jesus. Yet Flusser never claimed to have become a Christian.

There is an absolutely right way for Christians to assess, even to own, the Jewish values within the preaching of Christ. *But this cannot come with an agenda to de-Christianize Christ.* That is the factor that disqualifies, for traditional Christians like myself, so much mainstream or "liberal" Christian scholarship in the post-Holocaust style. Christian scholars who seem to enjoy the results of the third quest for the historical Jesus will receive only a faint hearing from traditional Christians. This is a given. The third quest is simply too eager in its skepticism for traditional Christians to receive it.

David Flusser, on the other hand, an Israeli scholar of Hebrew University at Jerusalem, was free of an anti-Christian agenda. He was free of negative feelings toward Christianity. This is clear from Flusser's affecting introduction to the second (1997) edition of his book. Flusser the Jew is an affirming portraitist of Jesus the Jew. Traditional Christians need to be informed of Flusser's views.

Chapter Three of my book, entitled "Jesus and John the Baptist," prepares the way for the main part of my argument. Notwithstanding the Jewishness of Jesus, his continuity with Judaism, Jesus' *dis*continuity with Judaism centers around his painful relationship with John the Baptist. John the Baptist was a preacher of imminent judgment. Jesus was not. With Jesus, the kingdom of God had begun, on earth, in history, but was yet to be completed and fulfilled. Jesus' message combined the already, or indicative, with the not-yet, or imperative. This combination became characteristic of later Christian thought. Jesus' eschatology was Christian!

In addition to his break with John, Jesus' rupture with his family needs to be factored in to the relation of discontinuity to continuity in his ministry. The break with his family is one of the few traces of a bona fide psychology in the Gospels' portrait of Christ. Now "psychology" has always been eschewed, eschewed sharply, violently even, by most New Testament scholars. How can we get inside such a figure as Christ? they ask. What evidence do we possess to paint in, let alone observe, the emotional colors of the man?

But we do have evidence. The several disturbing incidents and say-ings portraying distance and separation between Jesus and his mother and brothers would never have made it into the biographies we know as Gospels if their memory had not been so strong that it resisted the natural tendency in transmission to whitewash negativity. The trans-mission of religious texts usually works against any details that seem unflattering to the divine or prophetic figure. That these incidents and sayings are present within the New Testament, and that the skepticism of John the Baptist at the end concerning Jesus is also embedded in the text, are facts. These two facts provide clues to the discontinuity of Christ in relation to his context. We would be intentionally and deliber-ately resisting the significance and power of these striking texts, which are clues to an affirmation about him by way of a negation, if we did not recognize them as evidence for discontinuity.

Chapter Four, entitled "Jesus the Christian," is the heart of my ar-gument, the center of this book. At least five themes in Jesus' message are discontinuous, by definition, with Judaism. They are discontinuous by definition, rather than implicitly, with Judaism as a religion. This is because they all *name* the newness. They announce in words a new thing. These five themes embody the uniqueness of the historical Jesus. They do not contain it, but they do embody it. They detail the picture of a universal thinker, a voice for human community and for compas-sion based on a shared abject need for what could only be termed salva-tion. Salvation is the difference between *defeat* at the hands of human nature's inward "total depravity" — evenly, pervasively, distributed ac-cording to Jesus — and *deliverance* through the means of the friend to sinners. "Lay down your arms" is the summons of these five obtruding texts in the primary Jesus tradition. Each of them involves barrier-breaking and annunciating affirmations concerning human paralysis and divine responding.

Chapter Five is entitled "The Centrifugal Force of Jesus the Chris-tian." Centrifugal force is energy proceeding from the center out, in all directions, as the center whirls and spins. The discontinuous religious dicta of Jesus are the centrifugal vitality and force behind the movement that became the Christian church. The message of Christ was not the creation of Christians subjectively after Easter, nor was it the creation of St. Paul. Early Christian interpreters applied it and enlarged it, but they did not create it. The core of Christianity's worldview — compassion for perpetrators as well as victims; hope for new life in the face of the most far-gone circumstances; healing and comfort for the sick; criticism of the formal and superficial in favor of the material and substantial; inwardness and attention to motive; solidarity with sufferers and excluded people — these are all recognizable in the teachings of Jesus. Chapter Five derives the main dynamic themes of the Christian religion from the dissonant remembered words of the human historic Jesus.

A few terms or paradigms need to be mentioned, since they occur frequently in the text. *Continuity* and *discontinuity* are vital words. If an idea is continuous with another, it follows the same logic and grows from the same soil. An idea that is discontinuous with another idea breaks with that idea and grows into a very different tree. *Dissonance* and *dissidence* are important words, for they enhance and expand the idea of the discontinuous concept.

Particularity and *universality* are also important words. A particular word is correct and apt for a specific, local, concrete situation. A particular is Second Temple Judaism, or the Protestant Reformation of the sixteenth century. A universal, on the other hand, is an idea that speaks to every locale and situation. A universal applies to everybody, in every time and place. There are no exceptions or special cases in the application of a universal. If there is one single exceptional case, the universal ceases to be.[12]

Eschatology refers to the last word and development, or "end time," of human history. Eschatology is the final resolution of everything that has ever happened before. An imminent eschatology, such as John the Baptist preached, understands the end or last act to be coming

---

12. This is Immanuel Kant's description of the "categorical imperative": "I ought never to act except in such a way that I can also will that my maxim should become a universal law." See *The Groundwork of the Metaphysic of Morals,* trans. H. J. Paton (New York: Harper Torchbooks, 1964), p. 70.

soon. It is within view. An open-ended or delayed eschatology, such as Jesus preached, means that the end will surely come, but no human being knows when. Everyone is waiting, and we are required by reality to recognize the waiting.

A *centrifugal* or implicit idea is an idea that has not yet been stated in words but is pregnant within a manner of speaking or expressing. It is an idea that will develop, certainly and logically, from an earlier idea. But it will not come to complete expression until later.

Finally, *context* is the framework in which a person lives or an event takes place. To *decontextualize* a person or event is to take it out of its original setting and place it against another or larger background.

The Historical-Jesus Problem

The "never-ending story" of Christian students' attempts to get close to Jesus Christ as he really was has been told well and effectively in many places. Bishop Stephen Neill told it well, with Tom Wright, in *The Interpretation of the New Testament, 1861-1986* (Oxford and New York: Oxford University Press, 1988). John Riches narrated it well for the twentieth century in *A Century of New Testament Study* (Cambridge: Lutterworth Press, 1993). Every New Testament interpreter has got to know the lines of the road on which he or she is traveling, all the main planks and feeder routes, too, in order to do original work. Otherwise you find yourself repeating, almost even word for word, someone else's work from the past.

You have to know where the work has been done in order not to be destined to study for decades only to manufacture repetition and make the same old mistakes down the same old blind alleys.

Because I see this book as a continuation, within the twenty-first century's new context of a Jesus bound in close continuity to Judaism, of the second quest for the historical Jesus, I shall outline the three quests that have gone before, but all in light of the present post-Holocaust atmosphere of thought.

The discontinuity of Jesus with his surrounding religious world, and the continuity of his ideas with later Christianity, have become keys for me to understanding his contribution. Christ's discontinuity with his past and his continuity with Christianity's future become the lens through which the agendas and struggles of the last one hundred fifty years can be observed and summed up. What follows is a review of the three quests for the historical Jesus as magnified through the glass of continuity and discontinuity, and further through the lens of post-Holocaust Christian theology.

The First Quest for the Historical Jesus

The first quest for the historical Jesus began with two German Protestant Enlightenment thinkers or *philosophes,* Samuel Reimarus (1694-1768) and Gotthold Ephraim Lessing (1729-1781). Against the background of an assumed triumph of (God-given) human reason in the interpretation of religious texts and religious history, Reimarus and Lessing disclaimed the miraculous in the narratives of the Bible, and, most importantly for our purposes, in the Gospel histories of Jesus. For Reimarus and Lessing, the ministry of Jesus, the inspired sage, must by definition have been discontinuous with superstition and also discontinuous with the supernatural and miraculous. On the other hand, Christ's ministry must have been continuous with reasonable recollections concerning a reasonable historical figure.

Once the naturalistic anti-supernatural method had been prescribed by Reimarus and Lessing, together with others, several steps were to be taken in the creation of Jesus' new portrait by the first quest. One step, awesomely controversial at the time, was the biography of Christ written by David Friedrich Strauss (1808-1874).[1] This biography left out the miracles and glossed over the resurrection. Another step, hidden from public view at the time and still controversial today, was a "Gospel" of Jesus' life edited by Thomas Jefferson (1743-1826).[2] This se-

---

1. The novelist George Eliot translated the first English edition of Strauss's book in 1846. See *The Life of Jesus, Critically Examined,* ed. and trans. Marian Evans (St. Clair Shores, Mich.: Scholarly Press, 1970).

2. Thomas Jefferson, *The Life and Morals of Jesus of Nazareth. Extracted Textually*

lection of stories and teachings from Matthew, Mark, and Luke omitted the miracles and the resurrection, as well as many "religious" sayings of Christ, such as those concerning hell and the second coming. Many "ethical" dicta of Jesus were admiringly included by the American president, though not all.[3]

A third step in the first quest's long march to present a reasonable portrait of Christ was a biography by the Frenchman Ernest Renan (1823-1892).[4] Like Strauss's life, this biography, artful and even beautiful, influenced English "Free Thinkers" such as George Eliot (1819-1880) and the poet Robert Browning (1812-1889). Again, the result of these culled portraits from the Gospels was a Jesus of universal moral stature, but not a divine figure or bearer of revelation.

The Jesus of Strauss and Jefferson and Renan was also not an exclusive or particular thinker. He was high in the pantheon of great men like Confucius, Plato, and the Buddha. But he was not an avatar or a new Moses or another Muhammad. His achievement was continuous with humane wisdom but discontinuous with concepts of salvation and messiahship. The Jesus of the first quest was discontinuous with traditional religious Christianity and also with orthodox Judaism, al-

---

from the Gospels of Matthew, Mark, Luke and John (New York: The Eakins Press, no date).

3. In later life Thomas Jefferson changed his attitude towards the Christian church. His change of mind is documented in James H. Hutson's *Religion and the Founding of the American Republic* (Washington, D.C.: Library of Congress, 1998).

Thus the Rev. Ethan Allen, rector from 1823 of Christ Church (Episcopal) in the District of Columbia, told this revealing story, which is supported by evidence in the President's account books. Jefferson, according to Allen, "was walking to church one Sunday with his large red prayer book under his arm when a friend querying him after their mutual good morning said which way are you walking Mr. Jefferson. To which he replied to Church Sir. You are going to Church Mr. J. You do not believe a word in it. Sir said Mr. J. No nation has ever yet existed or been governed without religion. Nor can be. The Christian religion is the best religion that has been given to man and I as Chief Magistrate of this nation am bound to give it the sanction of my example. Good morning Sir." See Hutson, p. 96, all punctuation as in original.

4. *The Life of Jesus* (ET New York: The Modern Library, 1955).

though the relation to Judaism scarcely entered or influenced the discussion.

The first quest took an unexpected turn in the late 1800s. It was a U-turn. Johannes Weiss (1863-1914)[5] and Wilhelm Wrede (1859-1906)[6] turned the attention of the academic world, and by extension, the Protestant Christian world, to the *eschatological* theme in the ministry of Christ. Weiss and Wrede observed that Jesus' teachings are permeated by an intense and thorough conviction that the world's history is coming to an end and that his life and message are directly involved with the end.

It had always been apparent from the texts themselves that the end-time or eschatological theme was vivid in the Gospels. But the earlier phases of the first quest, rooted in rational and commonsense thought, had looked the other way. Weiss and Wrede were anti-liberal. They were passionately anti-liberal. They had contempt for the eighteenth-century ethical sage admired by their predecessors.

For Wrede and Weiss, the Jesus of universal brotherhood was a figure bound by projections of eighteenth- and nineteenth-century virtues: our "contemporary" in the sense of establishment values. They despised that Jesus! They therefore wished to heighten the strangeness of Christ, his *alien* character, and thus break his "continuity" with liberal thought. Weiss and Wrede were not particularly interested in the Jewish component of Jesus, but they were at pains to underscore the non-Western, non-rational, non-scientific element. There is a violence, an Oedipal violence, in these men's attack on the Jesus of their fathers. They were trying with all their strength to unhorse the previous generation. Johannes Weiss, in fact, who knew what he was doing, apparently waited until his distinguished father-in-law died before he published his own arguments. Was it under pressure from his wife?

Next came Albert Schweitzer (1875-1965), a scholar better known now for his medical mission at Lambaréné. Schweitzer poignantly perceived

5. Weiss's groundbreaking book was his 1892 *Die Predigt Jesu von Reiche Gottes* (ET: *Jesus' Proclamation of the Kingdom of God,* 1971).

6. Wrede's most influential book was *Das Messiasgeheimnis in den Evangelien* (ET: *The Messianic Secret,* 1971).

the impossibility of maintaining a "liberal" or Jeffersonian Jesus in the face of Christ's irritating futurism. Schweitzer could devise no way of combining these two sides of the man, the humane universal ethicist and the apocalyptic prophet. Finally, the theologian stood speechless before a failed man of God, twisting in complete defeat on a Roman cross.

With Albert Schweitzer, the whole project, the entire first quest for the historical Jesus, came crashing down.[7] That is not an overstatement. Schweitzer's 1906 book *The Quest of the Historical Jesus* is a kind of eulogy for the first quest. The last paragraphs of his book are justly famous. I quote them here:

> Jesus of Nazareth will not suffer himself to be modernized as an historical figure. He refuses to be detached from his own time. . . . He will no longer be a Jesus Christ to whom the religion of the present can ascribe its own thought and ideas. . . . Nor will he be a figure which can be made by a popular historical treatment as sympathetic and universally intelligible to the multitude. . . . The historical Jesus will be a stranger and an enigma to our time. . . .
>
> He comes to us as One unknown, without a name, as of old, by the lake-side. He comes to those men who know him not. . . . He commands. And to those who obey Him, whether they be wise or simple, He will reveal Himself in the toils, the conflicts, the sufferings which they shall pass through in His fellowship, and, as an ineffable mystery, they shall learn in their own experience who He is.[8]

Though affectingly and poetically stated, these sentences expressed *débâcle*. They summarized the complete defeat of the first quest for the historical Jesus.

---

7. Martin Kähler's 1892 essay collection entitled *The So-Called Historical Jesus and the Historic, Biblical Christ* also played an important role in the first quest's demise.

8. *The Quest of the Historical Jesus: A Critical Study of Its Progress from Reimarus to Wrede* (New York: Macmillan, 1968), p. 403.

Albert Schweitzer and his generation of European New Testament scholars, together with their many North American students, who soon populated the faculties of our mainstream divinity schools and liberal arts colleges, completely lost confidence in the idea of understanding Jesus "as he really was." They gave up the quest. In doing so, they gave up their old faith, Schweitzer himself being at the head of the class. He became a Christian agnostic and remained so for the rest of his life. He never recovered, religiously, from the death of the quest.

It was the discontinuity, as these men saw it, the essential discontinuity of Christ's eschatology, which made them regard the distinctives or *novums* in his message to be absolutely foreign to the modern world. Jesus had become an alien figure to the twentieth century.

Continuity in relation to discontinuity is a good model for understanding any phenomenon. It lights the distinctiveness or uniqueness of a thing, as well as its invariably derivative side. Thus I married my wife, but not her family. When I observe her family, I think I am able to observe the traits she has in common with them. No person is the way she or he is by accident or spontaneously. On the other hand, I have, like Mr. Darcy in *Pride and Prejudice,* an eye for the specialness of the woman I love, the qualities that make her different and unique in my eyes. She is not her mother, nor is she her sister. She is not her father, nor is she her brother. She came from them and has much in common with them. But the difference is what I love finally. The difference, or the difference as I see it, is what counts. This is an axiom of life.

It is the same for the Jesus quest. One is always looking for the specific or unique value of the man, his essence and thus the essence of the religion that carries his name. If one values the person, or wishes to, then the aspect of discontinuity is always more important than the aspect of continuity. For if the continuity overwhelms the discontinuity, then naturally the focus should shift to the source from which the continuity derives.

Originality, or creativity, is the thing in the history of ideas. Thus if Christ's continuity with Second Temple Judaism outdistances in extent and penetration his discontinuity with it, then our inevitable honest focus of interest should not be on Jesus, but rather on the root from which he came. Our focus should change. It should change from Jesus himself to Second Temple Judaism. If Jesus was first and foremost a first-century Jew in his thinking rather than a Christian, then the arrow of investigation has to point to first-century Judaism. That should be the proper first and more important object of study.

Christian New Testament scholars who regard Christ's continuity with Judaism to be greater than his discontinuity with it will inevitably discover themselves to be backing away from Jesus. They do this, in fact. They discern the seeds of nascent earliest Christianity in the real soil where they are definitely to be found. They therefore give up the quest for Jesus, or at least the quest in its character of first importance, because they have been looking in the wrong place. They begin to look in the *right* place, which is the documents and history of Second Temple Judaism.

The first quest for the historical Jesus shipwrecked, literally broke apart, on the discontinuity between acceptable standards of ethical rational thinking and the seemingly incredible links of Jesus the preacher to vivid apocalyptic ideas. The continuity broke down in face of the discontinuity. The first quest came to see too much discontinuity in him to make out a continuing or palatable picture of Jesus Christ for today. The first quest concluded, sadly, that the historical Jesus was unknowable.

The Second Quest for the Historical Jesus

After a lull of over fifty years, the urge, or need, to say something constructive about Jesus as he really was broke through to the surface again, as it had to do, at least for traditional Christians and traditional Christian theologians. It surfaced at a very specific time and place: at a reunion of theologians and pastors who were alumni of the University of Marburg, Germany, on October 20, 1953. On that day a lecture was given entitled "The Problem of the Historical Jesus."[9] The lecture was

9. The lecture was later published as "Das Problem des historischen Jesu" in Käsemann's *Exegetische Versuche und Bemerkungen,* Band I (Göttingen: Vandenhoeck

delivered by Ernst Käsemann (1906-1998), then a professor of New Testament at the University of Göttingen.

Käsemann was trying again to say something about Jesus. His fresh attempt became extremely influential. Why did he make this new attempt, for he was as well aware as anyone possibly could be of the complete failure of the first quest to achieve lasting results? Why did Käsemann announce the start of a new season of excavation, the opening of a new dig?

The reason behind Ernst Käsemann's proposal was his personal desire to separate himself from his celebrated Marburg teacher, Rudolf Bultmann. Käsemann wished to consolidate Bultmann's thinking about Jesus while at the same time distancing himself from it. This birth pang of the second quest for the historical Jesus, which was in fact a declaration of independence by Ernst Käsemann in relation to Rudolf Bultmann, requires some explanation for the common reader; but not too much explanation, for it is a lengthy and quite complicated chapter in the history of twentieth-century New Testament research. It requires some explanation, nevertheless, because an important point was in play.

Rudolf Bultmann (1884-1976) had argued in 1926[10] that almost nothing could be said, from an objective historian's point of view, about the life and authentic teachings of Jesus. Bultmann had several reasons for announcing this with such certainty, but his book was presumptive in the way it presented radical results as certain and therefore beyond discussion or criticism. Bultmann accepted the death of Jesus-studies as having taken place at the end of Schweitzer's time. Bultmann emphasized only the point that the wild eschatological sayings of Christ had been represented by Schweitzer, and by Wrede and Weiss, accurately.

Several years later, but long after Bultmann had finished supervising Käsemann's New Testament doctorate at Marburg,[11] Bultmann

---

& Ruprecht, 1960), pp. 187-214 (ET: "The Problem of the Historical Jesus," in *Essays on New Testament Themes* [Philadelphia: Fortress Press, 1982], pp. 15-47).

10. *Jesus* (ET: *Jesus and the Word* [New York: Scribner, 1958]).

11. *Leib und Leib Christi. Eine Untersuchung zur paulinischen Begrifflichkeit* (Tübingen: Mohr/Siebeck, 1933).

produced a book entitled *Primitive Christianity in Its Contemporary Setting*. There Bultmann included a chapter on the preaching of Jesus that gave considerably greater hope to any who were still interested in investigating Jesus as he really was.[12]

Käsemann agreed with a great deal that Bultmann said in the later book and also in other published lectures and essays. Like his teacher, Käsemann agreed that Jesus' eschatology was vital to his preaching of the kingdom of God. Käsemann saw that considerable fields of early Christian theology, St. Paul's letters in particular, had grown from the seed of apocalyptic.

Käsemann, like Bultmann, was a Protestant theologian who would not and could not detach his New Testament research from his larger systematic theological concerns. All of these concerns had been affected by their experiences of Nazism in the years from 1933 to 1939. As postwar theologians, Käsemann and Bultmann had been affected not so much by the Holocaust, which was still a new and unexplored theme in Europe in the early 1950s, as by their experience of being Confessing Church pastors in resistance to Adolf Hitler.[13] Käsemann saw certain

12. The chapter was entitled "The Proclamation of Jesus" and is found on pages 71-79 in R. H. Fuller's translation: *Primitive Christianity in Its Contemporary Setting* (New York: Meridian Books, 1957).

Although the influence of existential philosophy is strong within the last paragraphs of the chapter, and although Bultmann saw Jesus as a Jew and not a Christian, the implication of his approach is very definitely to heighten the discontinuity of Jesus' teaching and self-understanding in relation to Judaism.

13. The story of Käsemann's resistance to Nazism is printed in the December 1998 issue of *Transparent. Zeitschrift für die kritische Masse in der Rheinischen Kirche* (12th Year, No. 52). This biographical collection of documents, prepared just after Käsemann's death, is entitled: "Ernst Käsemann: Résistez! Nachfolge des Gekreuzigten führt notwendig zum Widerstand" (ET [Paul Zahl]: Ernst Käsemann: Resist! Following the Crucified Leads Necessarily to Resistance).

As a Protestant pastor in Gelsenkirchen-Rotthausen, Käsemann joined the Confessing Church and preached against the National Socialist compartmentalization of Christianity from politics. He was imprisoned by the Gestapo. Later, he quit the Confessing Church because he thought it wasn't radical enough!

On October 31, 1996, Käsemann wrote me the following interpretation of his resistance:

strengths in Christ's eschatology, strengths and virtues even for the contemporary world. He saw Jesus' apocalyptic as a resource for contemporary culture, shocked as it had been to the core by the crisis of the Second World War. He was not alienated or intimidated by the "foreignness" of Christ's preaching. Rather, Käsemann, who had had to crawl over piles of corpses, identified with it.

Ernst Käsemann was permeated, moreover, by the "early" Martin Luther.[14] He wished if possible to draw a line from Christ's and St. Paul's understanding of the good news of the coming kingdom of God to the Reformation's word concerning justification by faith. Käsemann saw the preaching of the historical Jesus as the "word from the cross" (1 Corinthians 1:18) *par excellence.*

Scholarship at the level of intelligence such as Bultmann's and

---

Whoever took part in the German Church struggle was a very individual partisan. I was one, too. I stood in the pulpit and right in front of me, in the gallery and below in the chancel, sat the Gestapo and the Nazis. You won't believe how much of an individual I felt then!: To preach heaven and to have hell right before your eyes in the person of its legates. . . . A thousand listeners were asked, at the highest pitch of individuality, to what end they were listening. . . . We represented our Lord and we risked His cross. We were called revolutionaries and were dealt with accordingly. But the kingdom of God is revolutionary! The Old Adam dances with himself, by himself — godless. (ET, PZ)

This moving letter of Käsemann's was dated "Reformation Day 1996."

14. A theological break or departure is sometimes discerned within Luther's scholarship between the "early" Luther and the "later" Luther. The idea is that the Reformer started with a view of the gospel that stressed spiritual warfare, the principalities and powers of the world against the authority and command of Christ, the overthrow of human strongholds by means of the exorcising power of God. The "early" Luther also stressed a theology of weakness and human handicap, i.e., the cross, in total contrast to a theology of glory, i.e., of victory. The "later" Luther moved more into ideas like forensic forgiveness and justification, imputation and also economic theories of the Atonement. The older he got, the more he began to sound like an orthodox Protestant theologian of the next century, the seventeenth.

That is the gist of the distinction between the "two" Luthers. It was a distinction very much alive and well in the period in Germany just after World War I when Käsemann was studying for the ministry.

Käsemann's, scholarship at the level of genius almost, involves full-field theories of human history. Bultmann and Käsemann were synthetic and wide-ranging thinkers. What was involved in 1953 was a powerful and grounded restatement of what Bultmann had already argued: that the preached message of Jesus can be reconstructed, and appreciated anew, if we affirm the eschatology. We have to affirm the passionate energy and dreadful imminence of Jesus' eschatology. To represent Christ's preaching with any hope of accuracy and sympathy, we have to begin by *embracing* its alienness. But there was more.

Jesus of Nazareth preached divine grace. He not only preached it: he lived it. "His words, his work, and what happened to him do point us towards keystones of the later gospel; and to that extent they can be used as criteria of this gospel. . . . Legalism cannot be made compatible with his specific self-understanding, nor theosophy and refusal to love one's neighbors with his belief in a gracious God, nor any *theologia gloriae* with his Cross. . . . I therefore emphasize with all the force at my disposal that for me Jesus was primarily the 'Evangelist' (without qualification), so far as that can be said before Easter."[15]

Käsemann felt able to state that Jesus was a Christian.[16] He here anticipated the biggest issue in late twentieth- and early twenty-first-century New Testament scholarship. He anticipated the anchor importance of Jesus' "Christianness" in relation to his Judaism. Käsemann wished to say that Christ expressed through his life, as it really was, that which Christians understand to be the entirely unearned favor of God to sinners and lawbreakers. In other words, Jesus taught and lived the grace of God.

Käsemann saw no difference between the way Jesus acted towards lawbreakers, unclean persons, and the like; and the characteristic of grace emphasized by St. Paul as being fundamental in the Christian savior and his saving act. Bultmann, on the other hand, saw the grace

---

15. Ernst Käsemann, *New Testament Questions of Today* (London: SCM Press, 1969), pp. 52, 56.

16. Käsemann's expressions concerning Jesus' "Christianity" are summarized on pages 110-14 of my *Die Rechtfertigungslehre Ernst Käsemanns*. See also pages 124-25.

of God as being a characteristic of God emerging from the church's time of reflection *after* Christ's departure. For Bultmann, Jesus was a Jew, a Jew only, notwithstanding his message of imminent judgment. The "Jesus of history" was a Jew. The "Christ of faith" was a Christian.

Ernst Käsemann saw a direct unity, one basic line, between the historical Jesus and Christianity. This involved the logic of Jesus' separation from Judaism. Käsemann's focus on the discontinuity of Jesus never left him.[17] He saw it as the major issue in the study of the New Testament right up to the day he died.

The second quest for the historical Jesus appreciated and endorsed the eschatology of Christ. It believed it saw important recoverable distinctives in the words and work of Christ. Coming out of World War II, which had been directly experienced by Käsemann as a nightmare, as a hell not beneath our feet[18] but as a clambering over hills of bodies in the P.O.W. camps where Käsemann himself endured the retributive hell faced by millions of German citizens at Zero Hour of the Nazi collapse, apocalyptic was as real to him as a theme in the gospel as the brotherhood of man had been to the earlier "liberals."

The great subjects of the second quest, therefore, were the continuity of the historical Jesus with Christian affirmations concerning the grace of God; discontinuity with the individualism and existentialism that had been popular modes of thought in philosophical theology before the Second World War; and the discontinuity of the historical Jesus with Judaism on the evidence of Christ's enacted paradigm of radical and universal grace that was thought to be dissonant and dissident in relation to the soteriology (i.e., ideas concerning salvation) present in most of the religious texts of Second Temple Judaism.

The last point was and is controversial. It is controversial partly because some scholars have argued since the late 1970s that Second Tem-

---

17. See his last short paper prepared for publication: "Protest!" in *Evangelische Theologie* 52 (1992): 177-78.

18. Käsemann understood hell as being the condition of our planet, the state of the race. See pages 166-68 in *Die Rechtfertigungslehre Ernst Käsemanns*.

ple soteriology was grace-filled and not legalistic.[19] I shall return to this question later, a "hot-button" question of the present day. The point here and now is that the second quest for the historical Jesus accepted the eschatology that the earlier generation had choked on. The second quest had no problem with a "non-rational" Jesus. The second quest heightened the discontinuity of Christ with his Jewish context, which in turn aided the continuity of Christian origins with later and especially Reformation theology.

What were the results of the second quest? They were Christ's discontinuity with Judaism in important respects; his continuity with Christianness or Christianity; and his continuity with the Reformation breakthrough concerning the grace of God.

What happened to the second quest for the historical Jesus? It is important to know. As one who was schooled in it during the late 1960s, as all of us were within the mainline churches and within mainstream American departments of religion, then more or less forgot about it for twenty years until coming up directly against the man himself, Ernst Käsemann, at Tübingen during the 1990s, I have had to ask myself: What killed the second quest? What sank it, what scuttled it? For there were lines of progress there. There was criticism and skepticism, yes. There was full acknowledgment of the debt owed to Weiss and Wrede. But there was also the aspiration to link up Jesus-studies with the inheritance of systematic theology. In other words, the second quest was synthetic. It was well grounded in four hundred years of

---

19. The key reactionary book on this line is E. P. Sanders's *Paul and Palestinian Judaism: A Comparison of Patterns of Religion* (Philadelphia: Fortress Press, 1977). This book is an extremely impressive case of one man's personal agenda given scholarly flesh. Sanders tips his hand early in his work. I have never recovered from spotting the admission of his agenda, which reads as follows: "The general Christian view of Judaism . . . as a religion of legalistic works-righteousness goes on, unhindered by the fact that it has been sharply — one would have thought, devastatingly — criticized by scholars who have known the material far better than any of its proponents. One of the intentions of the present chapter, to put the matter clearly, is *to destroy that view*." Emphasis mine.

Protestant systematic theology. The second quest was a courageous but not fantastic hope of understanding research on Paul in the light of work on Jesus. It was part Rudolf Bultmann, yet stirred in the immediate cauldron of 1945's *Zusammenbruch* and the horrors of the war that had led up to it. The second quest was a quest earthed in and deepened immeasurably by terrible experiences of life and death. The quest was founded from disaster.

What happened to the second quest for the historical Jesus?

One thing is clear: it disappeared. Its principal English-language interpreter, Norman Perrin, is largely unread today.[20] Rudolf Bultmann himself is considered much too Protestant or "Lutheran," although he is due for some rehabilitation. Käsemann himself is regarded today as hyper-"Protestant," even as reactionary, because he thought antithetically. Ernst Käsemann saw things in terms of either-or. For Käsemann, it was grace versus law, the powers of this world versus the powers of the kingdom, Moses versus Jesus, Galatians versus First Peter, Paul versus James. Käsemann's either-or approach, which stressed discontinuity over against continuity on almost every front, is not at all appropriate for most contemporary speculation concerning Jesus.

The last original piece Käsemann ever presented for scholarly publication, a piece that is short but maximally dense, was titled "Protest!" He gave a copy to me personally. "Protest!" took on a pastor-theologian named Jürgen Seim, who Käsemann believed had betrayed the Christianness of Christianity.[21] Käsemann thought Seim had contextualized Jesus so completely within the thought-world of Judaism that the Christianness of Christianity had disappeared. The old man never lost his thunder when it came to the discontinuities of Jesus with Judaism, and the Christianness of Christianity.

20. See especially his *The New Testament: An Introduction,* 2nd ed. (San Diego: Harcourt Brace Jovanovich, 1982) and *The Promise of Bultmann* (Philadelphia: Fortress Press, 1979).

21. Seim's piece, which so infuriated the author of "Protest!," was entitled "Zur christlichen Identität im christlich-jüdischen Gespräch" and appeared in *Evangelische Theologie* 51 (1991): 458-67.

What happened to the second quest? The answer is simple, but not simplistic. It was the Sixties. The late 1960s, with the student revolution that engulfed Europe in the spring of 1968 exactly two years before America's Kent State surge, changed the interests of mainstream university life. The student revolution of 1968 transformed the intellectual principles of Europe, and in this context, of European Protestant theology. Overnight, the famous Tübingen *Stift*, that university's ancient Protestant college, became a "nuclear-free" zone! Ernst Käsemann himself switched from Jesus-studies to "Ban the Bomb."[22]

Many of his contemporaries did so as well. When they awoke again, about 1975, like Rip Van Winkle, they were mostly old men. No one was interested anymore. Ernst Fuchs[23] was forgotten. Käsemann was forgotten. Only Rudolf Bultmann remained "relevant." But that was due not to his Jesus-book but to his "de-mythologizing" idea, which for Käsemann had appeared out-of-date as early as the 1950s. The Sixties swamped the lifeboat of historical-Jesus studies represented by the second quest.

The second quest for the historical Jesus died because it was overwhelmed. It was overwhelmed by the hurricane of May 1968. But Käsemann's harping on the issue of discontinuity, a concentration that never diminished with him, is still apt. It is still apt, especially, for the Jesus-quest of the post-Holocaust period, which we are in today. Käsemann's central concerns are a sharp retro-shock for New Testament scholarship. They are an unanswered rebuke to the third quest, a movement in full swing right now. For the third quest operates as if the second quest had never taken place.

22. See for example his essay "Bergpredigt-eine Privatsache," in *Christen im Streit von den Frieden,* ed. Wolfgang Brinkel, Burkhardt Scheffer, and Martin Wächter (Freiburg im Bresgau: Dreisam-Verlag, 1982).

23. Fuchs (1903-) was another important protagonist of the second quest. His *Studies of the Historical Jesus* (ET 1964) stressed Jesus' graceful table fellowship with the tax collectors and sinners.

The Third Quest for the Historical Jesus

The so-called "third quest" for the historical Jesus is represented in many people's minds by the "Jesus Seminar" of the 1980s and '90s.[24] But it is not synonymous with it. The "Jesus Seminar" was a group of scholars who adopted a set of skepticisms from the past history of New Testament study, and disqualified as non-historical and inauthentic many sayings of Jesus and also incidents from his life. The members of the "Jesus Seminar" were North American rationalists who strained out from the Gospels anything miraculous or supernatural. They were also a disunified group of partisans — or better, co-belligerent partisans — each of whom had his own particular idea of what Jesus had really been like. Revealingly, the first principal spokesman for the "Jesus Seminar" was Robert Funk, a radical student of Rudolf Bultmann's. I read his work back in the 1960s and early 1970s. Nothing comes from nothing.

The Jesus of the third quest has got to appear to be in continuity with contemporarily explicable or accessible types of what a religious teacher looks or sounds like. Thus the Jesus of the third quest might be an agrarian reformer, a sort of a populist organizer (Dominic Crossan); or a traveling "wise man," like an ancient Greek Cynic or an Asian sage with a rice bowl (Burton Mack). A Jesus from the third quest has to be someone who is identifiable and also understandable within the grid of our own late twentieth- and early twenty-first-century experience.

The whole thing comes out sounding like the first quest! This is because it is dealing with the same frustrating issue that was faced by Lessing and Jefferson, and by Schweitzer. We exclude the Jesus whom we cannot understand, of whom we cannot conceive. At the same time,

24. For a good summary of the aims and methods of the "Jesus Seminar," see Robert Funk's "The Jesus Seminar and the Quest," in *Jesus Then and Now: Images of Jesus in History and Christology,* ed. Marvin Meyer and Charles Hughes (Harrisburg, Pa.: Trinity Press International, 2001), pp. 130-42. See also Funk, Roy W. Hoover, et al., *The Five Gospels: The Search for the Authentic Words of Jesus* (New York: Macmillan, 1993).

however, we cannot or will not lose our Christian faith altogether. Our nerve fails us here, just when we ought, as Schweitzer did, to give up the ship of Christian believing. Most third quest scholars — though not all — pause before the courageous, desperate leap of Albert Schweitzer.

The issue of continuity versus discontinuity is the recurring issue of all Jesus research. The third quest cuts the lines of Christ's continuity with the elements in the traditional pictures that are unrecognizable to contemporary people. It then binds him in continuity with and conformity to accessible images in contemporary perspective. The whole approach seeks to stress the continuity and subordinate the discontinuity.

Yet the discontinuity is still the thing. It is still the heart of the matter. The discontinuity of something is always its key constituent. Experience of life tells us this. Why should not our research? Just as the first quest broke to pieces in light of the discontinuity, which in that case was the eschatology/apocalyptic of the Gospels' Christ, so the third quest breaks down in its allergy to discontinuous elements, any number of them.

In our particular post-Holocaust thought-world, the third quest is also suspicious of details in the picture that separate Christ from Judaism. The issue of Christ or Christianness as that issue which resulted in the "parting of the ways"[25] between the mother, Judaism, and the child, Christianity, is a presenting issue, or better, a presenting weakness, of the third quest.

What has happened is that a large number of books written about Jesus in recent years, books that are *de facto* a part of the third quest, have pressed the case for continuity between Jesus and his Second Tem-

---

25. The phrase came to the fore in recent New Testament scholarship through James D. G. Dunn's *The Partings of the Ways Between Christianity and Judaism and Their Significance for the Character of Christianity* (London: SCM, 1991).

For a more christological or traditional Christian treatment of the exact same question, see Martin Hengel and C. K. Barrett, *Conflicts and Challenges in Early Christianity,* ed. Donald A. Hagner (Harrisburg, Pa.: Trinity Press International, 1999).

For David Flusser's quite individual treatment of the "parting of the ways," see "The Jewish-Christian Schism," in his *Judaism and the Origins of Christianity* (Jerusalem: The Magnes Press, 1988), pp. 617-44.

ple context.[26] Some of this continuity is accurate and true to the facts. Jesus was a Jew. His ministry was situated almost wholly within Judaism. He was educated as a Jew and conditioned by Jewish thought. He was a man who carried out almost every aspect of his work with Jewish people and to Jewish people. That is unarguable.

But a cultural trend has taken over. A cultural trend has influenced the results of the third quest. Christian scholars, because of the Holocaust and because of Christian Holocaust guilt, fear that to speak of Jesus' discontinuity *with* Judaism inevitably feeds Christian triumphalism *over* Judaism. It is Christian triumphalism that has led in a straight line to the Holocaust.[27] So the Christianness of Jesus ought to be muted. Maybe his Christianness has been exaggerated by Christians. Maybe it has been painted in, retrospectively, even in the first moments of the "post-Easter" Christian community, to justify somehow a theological interpretation of Christ's death that turned a painfully obvious total defeat into an arbitrary apparent victory. Maybe Christ's Christianness was not there in the first place.

26. See the following major works: Geza Vermes, *The Religion of Jesus the Jew* (Minneapolis: Fortress Press, 1997); Bruce Chilton, *Rabbi Jesus: The Jewish Life and Teachings That Inspired Christianity* (New York: Doubleday, 2000); Paula Fredriksen, *Jesus of Nazareth: King of the Jews* (New York: Vintage Books, 2000); E. P. Sanders, *Jesus and Judaism* (Philadelphia: Fortress Press, 1985); John Dominic Crossan, *The Historical Jesus: The Life of a Mediterranean Jewish Peasant* (San Francisco: HarperSanFrancisco, 1991) and *Jesus: A Revolutionary Biography* (San Francisco: HarperSanFrancisco, 1994); John P. Meier, *A Marginal Jew: Rethinking the Historical Jesus* (New York: Doubleday, 1991); and N. T. Wright, *Jesus and the Victory of God* (Minneapolis: Fortress Press, 1990). There are many more.

An influential popular book on Christianity's Judaism is Marvin Wilson's *Our Father Abraham: Jewish Roots of the Christian Faith* (Grand Rapids: Eerdmans, 1989).

For a good summary of development along this line in the light of interfaith, i.e., Jewish-Christian dialogue, see Daniel J. Harrington, S.J., "Retrieving the Jewishness of Jesus: Recent Developments," in *The Historical Jesus Through Catholic and Jewish Eyes,* ed. Leonard J. Greenspoon, Dennis Hamm, S.J., and Bryan F. LeBeau (Harrisburg, Pa.: Trinity Press International, 2000), pp. 67-84.

27. Several Christian scholars have said this. Even James Dunn implied it in his 1992 essay, "The Justice of God: A Renewed Perspective on Justification by Faith," *Journal of Theological Studies* 43 (1992): 1-22.

Several degrees of damaged self-confidence among Christians are at work here. Perhaps it is correct that this be so. Perhaps the Holocaust, like the Law in Romans 3:19, *should* stop every Christian's mouth. Maybe Christians are required to concede the specialness of their man purely because such specialness issued in the destruction of millions. Maybe Christianity is finished, and Christians ought to migrate to Lambaréné. Maybe Christians need to act on the words of the Sinn Fein graffiti in Belfast, Northern Ireland: "Time to go!"

I am saying that context, the historical context in which New Testament research is done, conditions its results. Every age of quest for the historical Jesus has seen its own peculiar tensions reflected in the great tension between continuity and discontinuity.

In the eighteenth century, the discontinuity in Jesus' case had to exist in relation to the irrational; the continuity, in relation to the rational. Then his eschatology suddenly erupted out of the ground. Its brutal disturbance destroyed all hopes for continuity. So the first quest was dissolved. The first quest was dissolved by the apparent discontinuity of apocalyptic with modernity.

In the 1950s and 1960s, that same discontinuity, of eschatology and apocalyptic, fired the second quest, revealing a Jesus who must actually have preached in that way. Moreover, Käsemann and Bultmann both discerned continuity in the message of Jesus with the grace message of the Reformation. *Their* context, Käsemann's and Bultmann's, was the crisis — as it really had been for them personally — of the Confessing Church's failed crusade against Adolf Hitler. Their context was the horror of the ensuing conflagration. Käsemann said that the fingers of his generation of theologians had been burned by the purifying fire caused by the complete destruction of their country's misplaced hopes in a messianic national resurgence. Their hands had been burned to stumps in the bonfire of false messianic hopes burned away to nothing. Forced back to the Reformation they were, and forced to regard the fiery eschatology of Jesus as true to life! But the second quest was burned to cinders, in its turn, by the student revolution of 1968. The discontinuity of the Sixties exploded the postwar world of Käsemann and his colleagues. The scholarly results of their quest were buried in ash.

The third quest is now stuck on the same reef of discontinuity versus continuity. It is threatened, as the first quest was, by the tension and conflicting force of Christ's discontinuity in relation to his continuity. The discontinuity of the third quest is with Jesus as traditionally understood within Christian theology. The discontinuity is, as much as anything else, with the portrait of Jesus that animated the Reformation, the Reformation being an intellectual force against which many of the current scholars are in particular reaction.

The continuity of the third quest is with Christ's Jewish context. At one level, such continuity is unarguable, absolutely to be conceded, reflected upon, and absorbed, especially by Christian scholars. The problem is that the third quest leaves us a Jesus shorn of Christian distinctives, the magnetism of whom would be insufficient, alone, to explain the rise and persisting strength of Christianity. The Jesus of the third quest makes of earliest Christianity a variant of Judaism, a sect of Judaism accessible to Gentiles. This was Käsemann's passionate protest against it in 1990. Christianity, along the lines of the third quest broadly understood, is simply a way into Judaism for Gentiles, who can remain Gentiles physically while practicing Judaism spiritually. The third quest makes of the phenomenon of Jesus a too little thing.

The question that arises when a traditional Christian reads accounts of the enculturated Jesus is this: What was the fuss about? What is the fuss about? Jesus was a Jewish monotheist, heavily influenced by Hillel and others in Hillel's school of thought. The followers of Jesus made available some of the finer insights of Second Temple Judaism to non-Jews. Thus, St. Paul was not the announcer of a Christian gospel antithetical to the whole force of Moses' Law. St. Paul was rather the wise and forward-thinking dismantler of certain (superficial) barriers between Jews and Gentiles, such as circumcision and the dietary rules, with the result that many Gentiles could now share in the blessing of the Covenant. It is all of a piece. It hangs together. Christ's continuity with his original context brings down the Christology, lifts up the monotheism of Yahweh, and makes of Christianity, as it later developed, an awesome misunderstanding. The Christ of Christianity is

Bert I. Gordon's *The Amazing Colossal Man* (1958), mutated out of recognition and blown up a thousand times in size from what he really was.

My point concerning the third quest is that it, like the first quest, is all tied up with the issue of continuity. It is shaped by the continuity. And the result, for Christians, has got to collapse. This is because the continuity of an entity with its source, if its source is the primary thing, absorbs the interest inherent in the entity. The interest of the observer becomes redirected to the mother, away from the daughter. The daughter may be interesting, but nowhere near as interesting as her mother.

The point is obvious from life and literature. In *Great Expectations,* Pip's true love, Estella, has lived under the shadow and also the protection of Miss Havisham. Most of Estella's limits and fears have been shaped by the personality and also the woundedness of Miss Havisham. But Pip loves Estella! For this love to be fulfilled, she has to break away. She has to come alive in her own right. The dark curtains of the old house come down, the light pours through in a famous scene of love's liberation created by the author, Charles Dickens. Dickens understands the continuity arising from the past; the reader has the eyes to see the conflicted hand of the past. But Pip loves Estella. And the break, or breakthrough, occurs between Pip and Stella, not between Pip and Miss Havisham.

This is a crucial principle of interpretation. It is vital for cutting through the truths and half-truths inherent within all three quests for the historical Jesus. The first and the third quests break up against the discontinuity. They break up to the degree that they are uncomfortable with the discontinuity. The second quest was not quite so. But "circumstances beyond our control" — May 1968 — brought the second quest to an end. Within the pendulum swing of continuity and discontinuity, I wish to argue that there is a fruitful quest still pregnant within the New Testament material. That is the point of this book.

A Hermeneutic of Discontinuity

In order to review the determining issue in New Testament studies of the relative weight of the continuity of Jesus' teachings in relation to their discontinuity, the argument needs to take a further preparatory step. The question of comparison, the proportion or percentage of discontinuity as over against the proportion or percentage of continuity, is simply so important. Its implications are binding.

If Jesus brought to the thought-world of history a renewed or opened up perspective on Judaism, an approach that opened up the insights of a great religion to ethnic and racial groups beyond the nation to which it had been first addressed, then that redirects the *primary* intent, for Christians, towards the religious teachings of the Second Temple. If, on the other hand, Jesus imported something different in essence, an idea or ideas that were intrinsically new, creative, and heuristic for future development — centrifugal for culture — then Christians still do right to focus on him.

The hermeneutical principle seems obvious to me as a pastor-theologian. But it is not obvious, at least not obviously stated, in the research. This is the principle that if something is true in experience, empirically true and tested in experience, and for me, in pastoral experience, then it has got to be linked up with the results of research in the academic arena. If a concept is not true in experience, patently, universally, obviously not true in the observed experience of human life and loving, then it cannot be true in the world of ideas. Conceptual reality must cohere with empirical reality. Thus if discontinuity is the "rub" in everyday life and relationships, it must also be the thing in the life of the mind. The discontinuity of Jesus, if it is there in his works and words, has got to be the Christian's focus.

A relevant and disturbing example, by analogy, of the failure to integrate observation of life with concept is the idea of "solution to plight." That is a notion which has emerged from a school of thought known today as the "new perspective on Paul." The idea in play here, a notable contemporary case of an unsatisfactory interpretive principle, is important enough to apply by way of caution to historical-Jesus studies.

The concept of "solution to plight" was first proposed by Edwin Parrish (E. P.) Sanders, an American historian of ancient religion. Sanders's idea was that St. Paul's breakthrough in becoming a Christian consisted in his seeing a "solution," or answer, to a "plight," or problem, that was not previously felt or known by him. E. P. Sanders believed that Christ appeared to Paul in a vision on the road to Damascus. This religious experience, not prepared for by means of any anxiety or any presenting problem that might have worn Paul's spirit down to a point of openness or receptivity to the experience, *broke in* upon the man. Under the overwhelming influence of his epiphany, a sublime dramatic appearance, Paul had now to invent or project a "problem" to which Christ's death, life, and resurrection, as focused in his overwhelming appearance to Paul, were the "solution." Thus the "solution" — Christ's appearance — came first. Later, afterwards, came the "plight."

The "solution" was retrospective to the "plight." For Sanders, who believed that Second Temple Judaism was, *like Christianity,* a religion of grace and not of law (in Martin Luther's sense), the idea of "solution to plight" was the only way he could understand the *volte-face* of Paul's conversion, as well as the negative approach to the Jewish Law that the Apostle later presented in Galatians, Philippians, and Romans. Paul projected onto Judaism — falsely, wrongly, and with tragic consequences for the Jewish people — a "problem" related to the Law that only existed because of one *sui generis* experience he had had on the road to Damascus.

This idea of Sanders cannot be true. Sanders's "solution to plight" notion cannot be true. It flies in the face of all experience, all experience with people and human relationships, as well as all documented and felt religious experience. I have said this in several places,[28] for the principle is essential. It carries powerful and painful implications for much of our Christian scholarship. As a minister who has been ordained for almost thirty years, I have never ever met a person who be-

---

28. See "Mistakes of the New Perspective on Paul" in *Themelios* 27, no. 1 (2001): 5-11; "Understanding Luther and Faith Alone," "'Solution to plight'? Get Real!", and "Christ: The End of the Law," in *Modern Reformation* 2, no. 2 (2002): 20-21, 26-27, and 34; and "E. P. Sanders' Paul vs. Luther's Paul: Justification by Faith in the Aftermath of a Scholarly Crisis," in *Saint Luke's Journal of Theology* 34, no. 3 (1994): 33-40. Also reprinted in *Luther Digest* 2 (Summer 1994).

lieved he was moving in his life from solution to plight. It has always been the exact other way around.

Of course, there are instances of people who come to us as clergy, physicians, counselors, and even attorneys, who do not know what their real or true underlying problem is. Often a man or woman comes to you with a confused and inadequate understanding of what truly ails them. But they always come with *some* perceived "plight." They never come to us holding in their hands an answer before they have a question. "Solution to plight," as E. P. Sanders has made it a maxim in Pauline studies, following somewhat from Karl Barth, who also fell at one point into this odd way of thinking, is not true to life. *It never happens that way.* Ever. Therefore, the whole scholarly edifice of what is called the "new perspective on Paul" becomes incredible. It is not true in concept because it is not true in life. It is not true; therefore it cannot be true.

That example, from a parallel world in New Testament studies today, the world of Pauline interpretation and not the world of the historical-Jesus quests, is actually key for the three quests themselves. Experience, not to mention art and literature, witnesses to the fact that discontinuity, not continuity, engenders interest. Differentiation is what creates an object for study. Christ is interesting to the degree that he is the primary object and thus a worthy object of study. Why consider him apart from that? Why be interested in him apart from his difference? If he was "just" or even a little bit "more" than a rabbi in derivation from his teachers and the influences around him, then his level of interest for Christians shifts down.

This is not to deny the continuity of Jesus of Nazareth. No one, I repeat, emerges grown and fully distinct. No one. The story of Athena birthed in full armor from Zeus's brain is a myth in the modern sense of the word. It is completely untrue. Even as a metaphor, it is untrue. Jesus was a Jew, as I am an American Episcopalian Christian married with children. We are all, every one of us, in continuity with where we have come from. But is not our individuation still the thing? Romantic love tells us this universally. There are no exceptions to it in experience. *Vive la différence.*

It is wholly proper to relate the continuity of Christ to his disconti- nuity. Without the latter, Christianity collapses. Without the former, it is not credible in real time. But the former must overshadow the latter if Christianity is to survive, and thrive.

The Vulnerability of Christian Faith in Relation to History

There should be one final word of preparation before the quotient of Christ's continuity with Judaism is measured. This concerns the rela- tion of scientific investigation to theology. Within the first quest it was universally taken for granted that the results of the search for Jesus had everything to do with religious truth. To deny the miraculous element in Jesus' ministry was understood to threaten the heartstrings of Chris- tian faith. No one doubted that Samuel Reimarus, the first well-known protagonist of the Enlightenment quest, was a deist. He rejected the di- vinity of Jesus. No one doubts today that for most of his life Thomas Jef- ferson was a deist. He resisted the Christian idea that Jesus was a divine figure. Science, in its successful negative criticism of religion, was un- derstood to be consequential for religious faith, and doubt.

Two hundred years later, when the second quest came to life, it was still clearly understood that New Testament research and Christian faith exist in a relationship. Käsemann was a theologian to the same degree that he was a student of the New Testament. He said this again and again.[29] For example, he said he had problems with the miracle of Christ's bodily resurrection. This affected his faith, and his preaching. The effects were clear for everyone to see in connection with his contro- versial plenary address to the German Church Congress in 1967 at Hannover.[30] Ernst Käsemann doubted the resurrection, and that af-

29. He put this very plainly in a lecture given at Tübingen in 1963, entitled (ET) "Theologians and Laity." This is found in *New Testament Questions of Today* (London: SCM, 1969), pp. 286-300.

30. "Die Gegenwart des Gekreuzigten," *Kirchliche Konflikte*, Band I (Göttingen: Vandenhoeck & Ruprecht, 1982), pp. 76-91.

fected everything. The results of the Jesus-quest are determining for faith. They are not penultimate, nor are they neutral. To say otherwise is absolutely disingenuous.

The third quest has the same impact on theology. A Jesus in harmony with contemporary concepts of what a religious teacher is, becomes a Jesus who is *not other.* The idea of his Incarnation is diminished by the Agronomes-, Diogenes-, and Müntzer-prototypes deployed by the "Jesus Seminar" to make Christ understandable. More important than the third quest's eclectic continuity with such models is the other side of the quest: the emphasis on Christ's continuity with origins as being greater than his discontinuity with them. It is no good to break up the foundations of the theological distinction between Judaism and Christianity and claim that such is just the price of scholarship.

The percentage or proportion of contextualization imputed to the life of Jesus is the most important fact in the present and future of Christianity. If he did not light a new road, then there was no New Testament. If there was no New Testament, then there is no unique Christian means of relief for the human problem. If there was no atonement for original (i.e., universal) human sin, he was no divine figure. There is also no Trinity. The consequence of hyper-contextualization is a unitarian approach to Christianity, which becomes in its soft center a variant of Jewish monotheism that is open to non-Jews. Like the lurking fear underlying the 2001 film *The Body,* in which the skeleton of Jesus is supposedly found under a fruit store in Jerusalem's Old City, the cost of a Jesus who was not the First Christian is the collapse of Christianity.

And there is something more. A Jesus who has become amalgamated with Second Temple Judaism makes cheap Judaism's enduring protest against Christianity. If a contextualized Jesus makes of Christianity a lot of "sound and fury signifying nothing" (or a lot less than Christians thought it signified), then what does this almost entirely Jewish Jesus do to the Jewish protest? It makes that protest — the protest that "No, he was not the Messiah!" — seem empty and pointless. It becomes an awesome wound opened and reopened and reopened again, over centuries, in vain. It makes the Jewish protest into a Pyrrhic victory. I believe it is correct to say that the heavily contextualized Jesus of today is an insult to Judaism. Is that all there is? Is that all there was? Why couldn't we just have made up from the start?

A heavily contextualized Jesus makes Judaism's defining "No" hollow. It was in vain. A discontinuous Jesus does the greater honor to the mother. Jesus the Christian heightens the sublimity of Judaism's passionate negation.

I believe that the Jesus of history was a teacher both rooted in his context and distinguished — distinguishing himself — from it. The distinction is the thing, notwithstanding the bloodlines, and more, of continuity.

Jesus the Jew

The German language has a word that I wish the English language had. The word is *selbstverständlich*. It means "obvious" or "self-evident," and it describes a conclusion that follows naturally from a fact. It denotes a conclusion reached by logical extension rather than because of any further fact or extra piece of information. A conclusion is *selbstverständlich* when it derives without any possible contradiction or opposition from data that have been already accepted.

Jesus' Judaism is *selbstverständlich*. It is a fact about him that requires no defense or explanation. The fact is that Jesus was a Jew by birth who lived his whole life, almost every instant of it, in a Jewish setting. While he was aware of Gentiles — he talked about them sometimes — he made it clear that his mission was to Jewish people. While there are incidents recorded of interaction with non-Jews, particularly the Samaritans, who were really a special case of being Jews, and with the man known as "Legion," and certainly with the Romans at the end, the overwhelming conscious aim of Christ was to speak to Jews, to "his own."

Moreover, Jesus' students were all Jewish. His sparring partners in debate were also all Jewish, and all his sayings, parables, and teachings were directed to Jews. That Jesus was Jewish is *selbstverständlich*.

The question demanded of Christians is this: To what extent were Jesus' words original or new, and to what extent were they derivative?

What is the proportion of creativity in Jesus and what is the proportion of reflected wisdom?

History as Deciding

As a traditional Christian theologian, I am uncomfortable by definition with any portrait of Jesus that makes of him primarily or predominantly a teacher of received Jewish wisdom, no matter how wise such a person could be. This is said without apology. Such a Jesus, the bearer primarily of received Jewish wisdom, cannot carry my distinctly *Christian* hopes: my hopes for forgiveness of sin through him and for life after death because of him. A Jesus who is predominantly a teacher of received Jewish wisdom cannot support the Christology of Christianity.

E. P. Sanders understood this and acknowledged it in a 1990 lecture entitled "The Question of Uniqueness in the Teaching of Jesus":

> We should apply the rule that there is nothing new under the sun. "This little bit here," we may say, "is as far as we know without previous parallel in anything which Jesus' hearers might have heard, but the difference is marginal." This would be a fair statement to make about the double love commandments and numerous other parts of the teaching of Jesus. To go much beyond that is historically unjustified.
>
> The claim to uniqueness . . . is confessional; and it is very bad theology to hang a confession of faith on a verbal detail. Doing it creates bad Christology. This little detail and that are unique. . . . The basis is inadequate for the christological confession.[1]

Sanders believed that there is very little, save a possible detail "here and there," which one might regard as unique to Jesus as opposed to

1. E. P. Sanders, *The Question of Uniqueness in the Teaching of Jesus*, The Ethel M. Wood Lecture 1990, University of London, pp. 23-24.

similar to another Jewish saying in currency during his lifetime. Therefore, he said, stop the search for such details. Give it up. For even if you found something "here and there" that is unique, it would not be enough to build a religion on.

Lessing said the same thing 225 years ago when he cautioned that the universal truths of a religion should not be founded or constructed on conditional facts trawled up from human records. Lessing meant, like Sanders, that Christian Christology cannot be evidenced from history. It is a matter of faith, not facts.

For the traditional believing Christian, such reasoning is unsatisfactory. History is important to us. "For if Christ be not raised, then we are of all men the most to be pitied" (1 Corinthians 15:19).

Sanders's view, which sounds objective and matter of fact when you first read it, leads directly to the death of Christianity. If Christ is not evidenced from the historical Jesus, then the whole thing is a mental trick. Sanders knew this. Traditional Christians are by definition going to be uncomfortable with an approach that magnifies the continuity because the "facts" do not support the discontinuity.

Nevertheless, Jesus was a Jew. That is *selbstverständlich*.

What can a traditional Christian learn, or hope to gain, from the Judaism of Jesus? What is true for Jesus, whom Christians love and claim to know personally in the present, from his Jewish background? What is the extent of Christ's Judaism?

The Required Possibility of Changing Your Mind

During the twentieth century several Jewish scholars of great learning wrote books about the historical Jesus and Christianity. These included Leo Baeck (1873-1956),[2] Franz Rosenzweig (1886-1929),[3] Claude Monte-

2. See his *Judaism and Christianity,* essays translated with an introduction by Walter Kaufmann (Philadelphia: Jewish Publication Society of America, 1958).

3. See his *Judaism Despite Christianity: The Letters on Christianity and Judaism between Eugen Rosenstock-Huessy and Franz Rosenzweig,* ed. Rosenstock-Huessy (Tuscaloosa: University of Alabama Press, 1969).

fiore (1858-1938),[4] Martin Buber (1878-1965),[5] Samuel Sandmel (1911-1979),[6] Geza Vermes (1924-),[7] and Pinchas Lapide (1922-).[8] Each of these men admired Jesus, although Leo Baeck less than the others. Each of these men sought to understand him within his Jewish context. Each of them saw it as almost his life's work to say kind things concerning Jesus while conceding nothing to the traditional Christian view that the historical facts warranted the inference that Jesus was divine. Each of these scholars wished to be respectful of Christian feelings while at the same time giving nothing away to Christian Christology.

Of the seven authors I mention, only two of them ever considered becoming a Christian: Franz Rosenzweig and Martin Buber. One of them, Leo Baeck, was explicitly anti-Christian.[9]

4. Montefiore wrote prolifically about Jesus. A place to start is his *Rabbinic Literature and Gospel Teachings* (New York: Ktav Publishing House, 1970). He loved Christ's Sermon on the Mount.

5. See especially his *Two Types of Faith* (New York: Harper & Row, 1961 Torchbook edition).

6. Sandmel was generous to Christianity. He had a particular respect for, and friendship with, Rudolf Bultmann. A good starting place for Sandmel is *A Jewish Understanding of the New Testament* (New York: University Publishers, 1960).

7. Vermes is an interesting case, for he appears at first sight to be quite open to a somewhat traditional Christian picture of Jesus. But, he concedes nothing to Christology. His key books are *Jesus the Jew: A Historian's Reading of the Gospels* (Philadelphia: Fortress Press, 1981); and *The Religion of Jesus the Jew* (Minneapolis: Fortress Press, 1993).

8. See his *Jesus in Two Perspectives: A Jewish Christian Dialogue* (Lapide and Ulrich Luz) (Minneapolis: Augsburg, 1985); and *Encountering Jesus — Encountering Judaism: A Dialogue* (Lapide and Karl Rahner) (New York: Crossroad, 1987).

9. Baeck believed that two varieties of religion exist in the world, the "classical" and the "romantic." The "classical" is ethical monotheism, Judaism being the paradigm. The "romantic" is the projected need for a savior or deliverer, Christianity being the paradigm. Baeck understood Christianity to be a false religion.

Baeck's typology is represented provocatively and exactly in Stanley Kubrick's and Frederic Raphael's script for the 1999 film *Eyes Wide Shut*. In this film, the Gentile doctor romanticizes to the point of a dangerous obsession, an encounter with a prostitute, in which he thinks his life was saved by the conscious sacrifice of hers. The doctor's secular Jewish mentor opens his eyes, however, at the end to reveal that it was no more than a trick, to frighten and silence the doctor so he would not reveal

I have read all these authors and find them all, with the exception of Buber, to be unsatisfactory in their treatment of Jesus' Judaism. Why do I say this? For I am speaking as a traditional Christian now, trained both as a systematic theologian and New Testament scholar. Why do I resist every one of these extremely knowledgeable and gifted scholars? It is because they do not concede to traditional Christian readers the *one* thing, the only thing, that it is necessary for Christian readers to hear. They do not concede that it is possible, just possible — not probable, and certainly not necessary, but still possible — that Jesus of Nazareth might have been something like what Christians believe him to have been. In other words, each of these writers is unable to concede the possibility that Christians may be right about Jesus. In their closing off that possibility — and again, I am talking about the very least "give" — they make it impossible for traditional Christians, in our turn, to enter into real and not sham dialogue with them.

The point is important. It is frequently overlooked or minimized by "liberal" Christians. Liberal Christians accuse traditional Christians of being closed-minded on the question of Jewish-Christian dialogue. They fail to understand that such "closed-mindedness" could be turned around in exactly one minute.

My point has to do with how one hears another person's opposing point of view. If my opposite number in debate begins by saying that he disagrees with me but is nevertheless open to the chance, no matter how remote or slim, that I may be right and he may be wrong about the question, that takes the tension out of the debate. For me to be comfortable with debating my opponent, there has to be the chance, just one chance, that I might be able to win him over. I must offer him, by the way, the same chance. Debate requires the possibility, the most minute possibility, that each of us may be wrong and the other person right.

This point is decisive in discussing the continuity of Jesus. Conti-

---

an important secret. Raphael and Kubrick both intended their film partly as a commentary on Jewish wisdom in a Gentile world. Raphael revealed this in later interviews. *Eyes Wide Shut* is brilliant, a contemporary statement of Leo Baeck's thesis.

nuity here means the extent to which Christ was Jewish. Discontinuity here means the extent to which Christ was Christian. For the Christian believer, his or her Christology and thus his or her orthodox faith depend on the outcome. If Christ was primarily a Jewish figure, then traditional Christianity is fundamentally flawed. If Christ was primarily a Christian figure, who imported *novums* that broke through his context, then Judaism has to face a critique. Wrong or right, Christ's Christianity is a critique of Judaism. What I am saying is that for dialogue to take place, I must be willing, at least one percent of me, to question my Christology to its roots. The other person, my dialogue partner, has got to be willing to do the same.

Here is a contemporary example of this principle. Though separate from the issue of Christ's continuity and discontinuity with Judaism, the following example shows what religious dialogue requires in order for it not to be a fiction.

When the Roman Catholic or "nationalist" community in Portadown, Northern Ireland, challenged the Protestant Orange Order over its annual march the first Sunday of July from Drumcree parish church (Church of Ireland) down the Garvaghy Road, which runs partly through a Catholic housing estate, there was no dialogue. The Protestants would not meet with the Catholics, or the Catholics with the Protestants, unless conditions were first met that neither side was willing to meet. Then, unexpectedly, the Catholic "residents' association" won! The Parades Commission of Northern Ireland ruled that the Orange Order could *not* march down the Garvaghy Road.

Protestant resistance to the Catholic legal victory was immediate and overwhelming. A stalemate came into being that has made the first Sunday in July a day to be dreaded in Ulster even at the time of my writing. What to do? As it turns out, the Protestant parade has been turned back every year since 1998, including this past July 2002. The situation remains an impasse, for on the one hand, neither side has yet given away an inch to the other side. At the same time, the British government has sustained the nationalists.

But here comes a new idea. The former *taoiseach* or president of the Republic of Ireland, Mr. John Bruton, is a Roman Catholic. He is also the leader of a political party, *Fine Gael,* in the Republic. Here is what John Bruton said after the Parades Commission backed the Catholics or "nationalists" over the Orange Order in June 1998:

> "The (Catholic) residents have won a very important point. But I suggest they might now consider if the overall interests of the argument" (i.e., the Good Friday Peace Agreement), "and the broader nationalist interest in making the agreement work, would be served if there was a unilateral and uncalled for gesture of generosity towards the Orange Order by nationalist residents" (i.e., to allow them to march). (*The Times* of London, 30 June 1998)

This was an astonishing proposal on the part of John Bruton. It was not taken up by the nationalists, but it was an astonishing gesture all the same. Bruton invited the nationalist Catholics, whose identity is bound up absolutely tightly and for several centuries with their protest against the Protestant march through their area, to concede — in a way, to concede everything, for a moment. And why? Because they had already won everything.

I interpret John Bruton's call, unheeded as it was, as a clue, even a key, of great importance for the conduct of debate and disagreement in the context of strongly held positions. Bruton was inviting the Garvaghy Road residents to allow themselves to become Orangemen for fifteen minutes, the time it would take the Order to march by their houses. Had the residents allowed this, had they taken Bruton up on the "unilateral and uncalled-for gesture of generosity" he proposed, I believe the entire conflict would have changed character. They did not take him up.

Instead, the standoff at Drumcree remains in effect. I write in the fall of 2002, after a July in which there was once more bloodshed, as the Orangemen were turned away yet again at the entrance to the Garvaghy Road.

Here is the application of John Bruton's words to the Jesus question. The key to the question of discontinuity and continuity in the historical Jesus question is the depth of listening, on the one side, and address, on the other, that Jewish scholars and traditional Christian scholars are willing to extend to one another. It is axiomatic that a Christian of conservative or traditional belief, a person, in other words, for whom everything, absolutely everything — life, death, hope, forgiveness, any chance of life after death — depends on the unique identity of Jesus of Nazareth, can only hear, actually hear, the case for the "Jewish Jesus" if his own faith is heard by the Jewish interpreter as potentially universal. If the desire not to believe is ironclad, if the protest against Jesus is 100 percent a given — as opposed, say, to 98 or 99 percent a given — then the discussion lacks the most important thing. It lacks the possibility of any shift or give. This is what the Garvaghy Road has taught us. This is what the former *taoiseach* of the Republic of Ireland has taught us. Debate must include the potential for a change of mind.

I have to be willing to say that I will give up my Christology, which is my Christianity, if the grounds for it are uprooted by proof of Christ's overwhelming continuity with his context. In that case, I shall turn my attention, sadder but wiser, to the inspired trunk lines of Second Temple Judaism.

The other side needs to say the same thing to me. This is what I seldom hear from conversation partners who are coming at the Jesus question from Judaism. It explains why almost all Christian-Jewish dialogue is undertaken, from the Christian side, by "liberal" theologians.

Here is an axiom provable from the record, an empirical fact: Christians who are attracted to Jewish-Christian dialogue are almost all "liberal" in theology, tending toward a low or reduced Christology and emphasizing the first person of the Christian Trinity rather than the second.

My approach, extrapolating from John Bruton's olive branch to the Orange Order, asserts that traditional Christians, on the one hand, and Jews who are definitely not Christians, on the other, will not be able to come productively to the historical Jesus question unless the Christian partner agrees to be open to unitarianism and the Jewish partner to Christology.

I can think of few Christian scholars of conservative theology who would come to the conversation with a willingness, even just a theoretical willingness, to loosen their Christology if the evidence required it. I can think of few Jewish scholars with committed Jewish identity who would come to the discussion with a willingness, even just the most theoretical willingness, to soften their historic protest against the messianic identity of Jesus. But the truth can finally be found out only if just such a costly suspension of one's self, one's identity, comes into being on both sides.

An Intra-Christian Impasse

All of this is to introduce a discussion of Jesus the Jew. All of this is to introduce the significance for traditional Christians of the work of the Jewish Israeli scholar David Flusser (1917-2000).

Yet there is something more to say before introducing Flusser's unique contribution. To a traditional Christian — or better, a Christian with a high Christology — scholars who emphasize the continuity of Jesus with Judaism over his discontinuity with it but who come from Christian backgrounds are even harder to hear and receive than Jewish scholars treating the same material. I always ask myself, why is this author of Christian background so interested in arguing against the traditional portrait of Jesus as savior and messiah? What is behind his or her argument? I have to ask the question. This is because I am not convinced that scholars of religion are able to be neutral.

In the spring of 1990, I asked E. P. Sanders in a public meeting at the College of Charleston why he was so antagonistic to the Law/grace antithesis that runs through most of the older, Protestant interpretation of St. Paul. He told us of an experience he had as a boy growing up within an evangelical Christian culture in Texas. This experience enlightened him forever concerning the guilt-inducing reality of Protestant/evangelical ideas of sin, guilt, and Law.

Hearing Sanders was almost as much an epiphany for me as the moment of truth he had had as a teenage boy had been for him. I observed that Christian scholarship that dislikes traditional Christianity sometimes comes out of negative childhood encounters with conservative — read legalistic — versions of Christianity.

We should not be afraid to speak of the personal side of New Testament scholarship. Two years at Chapel Hill in the department of religion during the late 1960s, followed immediately by two years at Harvard College and then a further year at Harvard Divinity School, were grist for the mill. Without exception, every "liberal" Bible scholar I ever met came from a "conservative" Protestant/evangelical background. There seemed to exist a one-to-one correspondence between skepticism in approaching the New Testament and fundamentalism as an early influence being rejected. Oedipus, the myth of Oedipus, I whispered, as time and time again a "liberal Protestant" New Testament lecturer turned out to have had a "fundamentalist" or hyper-evangelical father who was a pastor or missionary.

Because of this, I have become skeptical of the results of Christian New Testament scholarship. I expect that all too often it hides a deep and even dark personal reaction to "old time religion." I am wary of such psychologically conditioned "results."[10]

In the question of Jesus' Judaism, a traditional Christian is going to have a hard time swallowing the results of scholars on the Christian side who flock enthusiastically, as opposed to ruefully and sadly, to a view of Christ that costs him his uniqueness. We are going to have a hard time, by definition, with a view of Christ that embeds him so snugly in his context that his individual lines and contours begin to fade.

The truly liberal act of studying the history of religions is rarely able to take place, because conservatives do not trust liberals and liberals ridicule conservatives. Behind it all is the myth of Oedipus the son in relation to Oedipus the king. This was always true in Protestant

---

10. I have to ask myself, incidentally, whether my own results are not just as vulnerable to psychological conditioning as those of authors against whom I argue. Was Ernst Käsemann thus a "father-figure" for me, whose advances I followed as a son? I acknowledge the question. In fact, Käsemann always summoned me to be independent. He even cautioned me at one point during the Tübingen years to come see him less often, so I could not be accused of being his *Schuler,* or "disciple."

theological scholarship in Germany, but was seldom acknowledged. Just study the fathers of the greatest names in German Protestant critical scholarship, and you will be amazed at what you find. Conservatives sired liberals.

Christian Defenses, Flusser's Concessions

I first encountered David Flusser's *Jesus* while at Tantur Ecumenical Institute for Theological Studies in Jerusalem. David Flusser was a scholar of the New Testament[11] who was of Jewish faith and Jewish background. He taught for decades at Hebrew University in Jerusalem. He was a member of the Israel Academy of Science and Literature and was awarded the Israel Prize in Literature in 1980. He was universally regarded in Israel as a person of priceless erudition committed to the study of Second Temple thought.

Flusser's 1997 preface to his *Jesus* book[12] contains a few sentences that opened me right up, a traditional Christian, to its main message:

> I readily admit that I personally identify myself with Jesus' Jewish *Weltanschauung*, both moral and political, and I believe that the content of his teaching, and the approach he embraced have always had the potential to change our world and prevent the greatest part of evil and suffering.[13]

In the same preface, Flusser explained why he was open to Jesus' message and not bound, as a religious Jewish man, to an anti-christological mindset:

11. Flusser had no problem with the traditional Christian nomenclature of two Testaments.

12. Flusser's other main book is *Judaism and the Origins of Christianity* (Jerusalem: The Magnes Press, 1988), sometimes referred to as the "Red Book." This is not currently in print, but his 1987 radio talks on the Israeli Army Network are: *Jewish Sources in Early Christianity* (Tel Aviv: MOD Books, 2nd printing 1993).

13. *Jesus*, 3rd edition (Jerusalem: The Magnes Press, 2001), p. 15.

As a boy I grew up in the strongly Catholic, Bohemian town of Příbram. Because of the humane atmosphere in Czechoslovakia at that time, *I did not experience any sort of Christian aversion to my Jewish background. In particular, I never heard any accusation of deicide directed against my people.* As a student at the University of Prague, I became acquainted with Josef Perl, a pastor and member of the Unity of Bohemian Brethren, and I spent many evenings conversing with him. . . . The strong emphasis which this pastor and his fellow brethren placed on the teaching of Jesus . . . stirred in me a healthy, positive interest in Jesus, and influenced the very understanding of my own Jewish faith as well. (emphasis added)[14]

David Flusser was Jewish, but had a "healthy, positive interest in Jesus." It is this "positive interest" that makes Flusser's work able to speak to Christians who hold a high Christology. I, for one, have learned more from Flusser, and have thus been able to correct my own mistaken Christian preconceptions concerning Jesus' Judaism, than from any other writer, Christian or Jewish, whom I have read during thirty-five years of study. It is therefore Flusser's Jesus whom I seek to present, critically, here.

Flusser's Achievement: A Jewish Jesus for Christians

According to David Flusser, Jesus was a Galilean Jew who lived most of his life in Nazareth.[15] His birth date is uncertain, but he was baptized

---

14. *Jesus,* p. 16.

15. Flusser feels certain that Christ was born in Nazareth, not in Bethlehem, and discounts most of the Christmas stories as legendary.

I do not accept his skepticism on this point. This is because the Bethlehem tradition is just so strong and so old. It was certainly as solid as a rock by the time St. Helena, the Christian empress, arrived in the 320s. Flusser's point in opting for Nazareth is that he wishes to emphasize the Nazarene — i.e., pious observant — background of Jesus in his early formation.

either in 27/28 AD or 28/29 AD by John the Baptist. He had four brothers and several sisters. He was addressed as "Rabbi" by children, and as "Lord" by his inner circle and by those who came to him in need.

There is a psychological element in his life that comes out in the conflict Christ experienced between his ministry and his family ties. Few mainline Protestant scholars have ever given an inch to the idea that the Gospels reflect a psychological or emotional note in Christ's split with his family. Mainline Protestant scholars are in the grip of an *a priori* fixed idea when they do this, when they stonewall the possibility of psychological facts in the Gospels' Jesus. They will not accept the idea of some degree of inwardness or emotional accessibility in the accounts from Matthew, Mark, Luke, and John.

Yet it is clear from his reception in Nazareth (Matthew 13:57; Mark 6:4; Luke 4:24), his strong words to his mother and brothers when they were looking for him (Mark 3:31-34; cf. Luke 11:27-28), and his words from the cross to his mother — parallel to his word to her at the Cana wedding as reported in John (John 2:4 and 19:26-27) — that Jesus broke with his family. Flusser is commonsense in his approach to Jesus' split with his family. It is in the text. It is there in force. And it is uncommon in any case that it would be reported, within the context of an agrarian society that prized blood relationships above all others and everything else besides, unless there were something to it.

Why would the incidents of Jesus' diffidence in connection with his mother have made it past the entrenched resistance in that culture to such diffidence, if those events were not impressed indelibly on the memories of those who had been with him? The natural processes of textual transmission would regard such memories as disposable, unless they were too widely known, too well remembered, and too impressive to be struck from the record.

Flusser understands the baptism of Jesus by John the Baptist to have been the decisive moment that inaugurated his mission. Moreover, Jesus' relations with John, and in particular with John's imminent eschatology, were fundamental for his self-definition. Christ's relations with John clarified his concept of what he was doing. Had it not been for his relation to John, his proclamation would have been static and uncreative. I will return in the next chapter to the question of Jesus' eschatology in relation to John's.

From a traditional Christian perspective, Flusser is thin when he comes to the issue of Jesus and the Law. It is important to Jewish interpreters of Christianity, and especially to Jewish interpreters who are sympathetic, as Flusser is, to Jesus, that the Jewish Law remain in principle uncriticized and thus undamaged by the teachings of Jesus.[16] The assault on the Law that Christian interpreters over the centuries have ascribed to Jesus is threatening to the religion of Judaism on almost any account. Jesus' debate with the "teachers of the Law" is softened by recent interpreters on the Christian side, and is downplayed by almost all interpreters on the Jewish side.

Flusser is uncomfortable with the note of antithesis and confrontation in relation to the Law that occurs in the Sermon on the Mount. On this front, he concedes one point and one point only: "Jesus emphasized the moral side of life in preference to the purely formal side of legal observance" (p. 64). As a whole, however, Jesus' understanding of the Law was rooted in universal non-sectarian Judaism. Thus Jesus was closer to the Pharisees than Christians often believe, yet also highly critical of the Sadducees.[17]

Flusser's Jesus did not oppose the Law of Moses. "The germ of revolution in Jesus' preaching does not emerge from a criticism of Jewish law, but from other premises altogether" (p. 81). Flusser is no ally, therefore, to Luther or to other Reformation-minded interpreters of Jesus. Jesus upheld the Law, deepened it somewhat, but never opposed it. That is Flusser's settled view.

There *was* a revolution, however, brought by Jesus. The revolution brought by Jesus broke through at three points: his radical interpretation of mutual love, his call for a new morality in relation to the outcasts of society, and his new idea of the kingdom of heaven. These three breakthroughs, as Flusser understands them, are to be seen primarily

16. See, for example, *Jesus*, p. 75, note 43.

17. "Although not really a Pharisee himself, (Jesus) was closer to the Pharisees of the school of Hillel who preached love" (*Jesus*, p. 92).

in the parables and also in Christ's conduct toward lawbreakers and sinners. For example, Flusser believes that the command to love one's enemies (Matthew 5:44) is a stronger statement of Rabbi Hanina's teaching that a person should love the righteous but not hate the sinner. Jesus' word is a decisive step further.

Flusser does believe that almost every word reported of Christ does have some precedent or parallel within ancient Jewish thought.[18] At the

---

18. A note is necessary here concerning the Jewish parallels to Christ's teachings that were collected by the Jewish Christian scholar Paul Billerbeck. His once famous collection, known as the "Billerbeck," took the form of a commentary on the New Testament, and was produced in the 1920s.

Paul Billerbeck (1853-1932) was a Lutheran pastor of great erudition and also of Jewish background. His work attempted to place the words of Jesus in their Jewish context by collecting every known parallel to his teaching from Jewish literature, that is, from the teachings of the rabbis who preceded him and from those in antiquity who also immediately followed him.

There have been two primary objections to Billerbeck's amazing achievement. Incidentally, I have read much of it, in the German language, and have read almost every word of the first volume, which is his Matthew commentary: *Das Evangelium nach Matthäus. Erläutert aus Talmud und Midrasch* (Munich: C. H. Beck, 1926; 9th unchanged edition, 1986). I only say this because some scholars who dismiss Billerbeck have not read a word of him and take their opinion concerning him from E. P. Sanders, who did read him, or at least read Billerbeck's important excursus on Old Testament religion in relation to New Testament soteriology.

The two common objections to Billerbeck's work are as follows. First, it is chronologically all over the place. That is, it compares Jesus' words with Jewish sayings that both predate him and post-date him. How, it is objected, can ideas that post-date Christ be used to elucidate or anchor his own conceptions "as they really were"? The objection is fair. Even now, teachers and students at Hebrew University in Jerusalem are preparing a new "Billerbeck." This will classify the Jewish parallels by date and omit most later similar sayings. On the other hand, later rabbinic sayings that touch on Christ's concerns should not be totally read out of the package. This is because they were sometimes expressed in opposition or deliberate correction to Christian emphases of the first, second, and third centuries. They may offer clues, important ones, to the way Jesus' ideas were being expressed by Christians in the post-70 A.D. world of Jewish consolidation. This is because the rabbis were concerned by that point to mark off their tradition from Christianity. You could say that later Jewish parallels are interesting to students of early Christianity because same time, the way it falls together in the teachings and life of this one man is unique. The combination of ideas in Christ's teaching, the radi-

---

they offer pictures of what Christ did not say, therefore helping us by way of negation to understand what he did say. Billerbeck would have confirmed this. His method, which was to pour all the parallels he could find into one mixing bowl regardless of date — although he always supplied the dates or approximate dates of the rabbis' words he quoted in relation to Jesus — is not totally fruitless. You can learn a lot about Abraham Lincoln and the context of his Gettysburg Address by reading the (generally dismissive) comments in the newspapers the weeks and months after the address was given. The same would be true for Jesus and the rabbis who were teaching against the new religion.

The second criticism laid against Billerbeck is a bigger fish. It is not a methodological or "process" objection. It is more fundamental. It is also relevant for this book.

The second objection to Billerbeck is that he wrote as a convinced Lutheran Christian and therefore brought to his work a bias concerning the discontinuity of Christ with Judaism, especially in the theme of grace over against Law. This conviction, or bias as it is now interpreted by E. P. Sanders and his followers, projected onto Jesus' supposed critique of the Law a Protestant/Reformation bias. This "Lutheran" projection made Billerbeck see discontinuity and negation where there really was continuity and endorsement.

Billerbeck's chief sin was the sin of reading Christ and his Jewish parallels through "Reformation spectacles." The offense, however, is even worse than that. He was a German Lutheran pastor who was also Jewish. Billerbeck was Jewish by descent. And in the pre-Nazi, pre-Holocaust context in which he worked, this did in fact weigh against him. It is well known that as a pastor of Jewish origin, he had to approach Hermann Strack of Greifswald University to get Strack's backing and the "cover" of his Gentile name in order for the book to be published. This is still a source of shame today for German scholarship, and makes Billerbeck's case a pendant to Gerhard Kittel's, the National Socialist's, on the other end. It is very sensitive and hard even now for German scholars to comment on Billerbeck one way or the other.

For American scholars of the third quest in the post-Holocaust context, Billerbeck is extremely problematic. He was too much of a Christian: Billerbeck saw the historical Jesus as a protagonist of Christianity, even in Second Temple context, rather than as a rabbi essentially. This insistence on Billerbeck's part that Jesus parted fundamentally with Second Temple ideas of salvation and sacrifice, repentance and rehabilitation, is unacceptable in contemporary perspective.

One day, in a period of greater confidence among Christians in Christology, calizing tendency within some of his restatings of the Law, the pastoral practice of his ministry, and most importantly, Jesus' break with John's eschatology of the kingdom: these together make his life's achievement unique.

Flusser sees in Jesus' attitude to social outcasts some elements of Essene teaching. "The profoundly human beatitudes of Jesus breathe the spirit of the Essenes, who, although less hostile in his times, still had not discarded their misanthropic theological impulse. It should be noted in this connection that radical sects can often be quite amiable."[19]

An extraordinary paragraph is found at the end of Flusser's chapter on Jesus' ethics. It is worth quoting almost in full:

> Jesus' concept of the righteousness of God . . . leads to the preaching of the Kingdom in which the last will be first, and the first last. It leads also from the Sermon on the Mount to Golgotha where the just man dies a criminal's death. It is at once profoundly moral, and yet beyond good and evil. In this paradoxical scheme, all the "important" customary virtues, and the well-knit personality, worldly dignity, and the proud insistence upon the formal fulfilment of the law, are fragmentary and empty. Socrates questioned the intellectual side of man. Jesus questioned the moral. Both were executed. Can this be mere chance? (p. 102)

It is not enough for David Flusser to recognize a revolution in Jesus issuing from his extreme version of the love command, from his association with social outcasts, and from an eschatology conceived in opposition to the Baptist's. All that is not enough for him.

Paul Billerbeck may come back into fashion. Despite his undisciplined chronology — which he nevertheless flagged in every case by giving dates to his texts — his work has done the world a service in showing where Jesus' ideas were significantly derivative and where also they were significantly creative.

19. *Jesus*, p. 97. See also pp. 98 and 101. I think the "amiability" he has in mind here is the kindness shown him in his youth by the Bohemian Brethren at the University of Prague.

For in addition to it, in addition to Christ's three revolutions in the context of Judaism, David Flusser wants most importantly to emphasize Jesus' "high self-awareness." This is Flusser's phrase (pp. 118ff.). It is his way of coming up to the dividing wall of Jesus' divine identity. For Christians with a high Christology, this is the most counterintuitive and astoundingly welcome theme in his entire thought, for in his life Flusser never seems to have left Judaism.

On the one hand, Flusser rejects the idea that Jesus conceived of his death as an expiation for sin: he was no "Christ of the festival" of a medieval sacred drama (p. 123). Because Jesus, for Flusser, wrestled with death to the very end, Flusser's "Christology," if we can use the word, is in Christian terms "Antiochene": it focuses on the humanity rather than the divinity. Flusser does not see Christ as a "Lamb of God, that taketh away the sins of the world."

On the other hand, Jesus believed that his death would not prove to be the end of the story. "The very stone which the builders rejected has become the head of the corner" (Psalm 118:22; Luke 20:17). Flusser comments, "This is Jesus' unequivocal 'Christological' utterance" (p. 122).

Flusser also believes that Jesus' use of the title "Son of Man" is an indirect admission of his messianic dignity (p. 131). He narrates in detail the clash of Christ, initiated by Christ, with the Sadducean temple hierarchy at Jerusalem. This clash led to his death. "Jesus' words and actions in Jerusalem precipitated the catastrophe" (p. 141). He was found guilty of blasphemy by a Sadducean court, which then manipulated Pilate, the corrupt colonial governor who was himself an anti-Semite, to get rid of Jesus as a political threat to Roman rule in Judea. "Jesus' tragic end . . . was the outcome of a grisly interplay of naked spheres of interest in the shadow of brutal antagonisms" (p. 166).[20]

Flusser ends his brief bravura summary of what is known concern-

---

20. To a traditional Christian, Flusser's "throwaway line" concerning the resurrection is also astonishing: "I am convinced that there are reliable reports that the Crucified One appeared to Peter, then to the twelve. Then he appeared to more than 500 brethren at one time" (1 Corinthians 15:3ff.). (See pp. 154-55.)

ing the historical Jesus with a sentence that leaves the traditional Christian reader unpayably in his debt: "Jesus' acute self-awareness cannot be denied, and I am convinced that he eventually embraced the conviction that he would be revealed as the Messiah of Israel" (p. 176).

It is no wonder that David Flusser's *Jesus* is seldom cited, either by Jewish scholars, to whom he appears too "Christian," or by "liberal" Christian scholars, to whom he appears too "conservative." He is willing to take the Gospels much more at face value, as innocent until proven guilty, as reliable texts of written reminiscence, than the majority of mainline Christian New Testament scholars. This combination in Flusser of conservative textual values, Jewish emphasis, and openness to Jesus as a winsome real person of history makes Flusser's work of unique significance in the present context of New Testament research.

As a traditional Christian with a high Christology, my personal resistance to a contextualized Jesus softens with every page I read of Flusser's *Jesus*. As a Christian who values the Bible per se and places it in a unique position within the history of literature, I can read his criticism of some "Christian" editing (i.e., anti-Jewish additions) in the redaction of Matthew and Mark with an open mind. As a Christian who is inevitably and naturally threatened by the Jesus of the third and first quests, I become more open to the post-Holocaust insights even of "liberal" Christian scholars because of Flusser's Jewish appreciation of Jesus.

In short, Flusser's affirmation of aspects of Jesus in the Gospels that are important beyond words for me as a Christian believer has the potential to stretch my Reformation-filtered Jesus over wide new areas of appreciation for his Jewish origin.

Jesus the Jew

What, then, should be said here concerning the contextualized Jewish Jesus, the historical figure who was continuous with his setting? What can a Christian interested primarily in the discontinuity say about Christ's continuity?

Jesus of Nazareth was a Galilean Jew related through his mother to a priestly family of piety and observance. He broke with her and also with his cousin John at the earliest stage of his call, which he "heard" as a call from God to teach about the kingdom of God. His views concerning the kingdom of God were the germ of an idea that came later, in the days of Christianity, to have implications for eschatology, anthropology, and soteriology. He also lived by his own desire among social outcasts and lawbreakers, signaling an approach to the Law that became centrifugal for the later Christian movement. He expanded the love of one's neighbor to include the love of one's enemy. Much of what Christ taught had parallels in Jewish writings of his own period and earlier. Some of what he taught was sharper, more extreme, and more pointed.

Jesus had a "high self-awareness." This led to trouble, which he brought upon himself, at the temple in Jerusalem. He was not primarily the victim of the Pharisees, but rather of the Sadducees. The Romans put him to death, but they and certain Sadducees together were the agents of his execution. He died believing that his cause would be justified and vindicated. There are reliable reports that he was seen after his death by former students and followers.

The Judaism of Jesus is *selbstverständlich*. But it contains within itself seeds of difference. Like all big ideas, Jesus' ideas began small, from seeds. But the seeds were nuclear. They bore within themselves the potential for chain reaction. The discontinuities of Jesus in history were centrifugal for Christianity.

• 3 •

Jesus and John the Baptist

It is a rule in the history of ideas that new concepts start small but are able to grow, like the seed in Christ's parable, into big trees (Matthew 13:32; Luke 13:19). Such a concept is the idea of the kingdom of God, as expressed in the Gospels.

It began as a tension with John the Baptist over timing and ended up as a kind of petri dish for every scheme that has ever been fashioned by people to hold hope for the future while also living in the present. Jesus' dissent with John led to one of the most creative ideas that has ever been birthed in the history of religion: Martin Luther's insight, from his study of Paul, which is known as *simul iustus et peccator*. This means "justified and at the same time a sinner," or, for us today, "loved yet at the same time wholly human."

Jesus' disagreement with John the Baptist concerning the kingdom of God was the germinating point for the whole Christian understanding of human nature in relation to the Law or imperative of God.

It is evident that John the Baptist came to the end of his life, as he awaited final judgment from Herod Antipas in Herod's fortress-prison at Mahasuerus, with doubts concerning Jesus' mission and calling. This is evident from a celebrated incident reported in Matthew 11 and Luke 7.

The disciples of John, who was in prison, came to Jesus on behalf of their teacher and asked, "Are you he who is to come, the Messiah, or do we look for another?" We know that earlier, in relation to John's baptism of Christ, John had hailed Christ as the one who had come from God, the Messiah more or less. Now, at the end of his own course, John was no longer sure.

The rupture — which may be too strong a word — between Jesus and John had to do with their differing timetables for God's judgment of the world. John believed that the great and terrible day of the Lord (Malachi 4:5) was imminent. It was coming *soon*. This is why he said, "Even now the axe is laid to the root of the trees" (Matthew 3:10). The dreadful day of final judgment was around the corner.

Jesus, apparently differing with John, saw redemption history, the big picture of God's engagement with humanity, in a more openended, transitional way.

To understand Jesus' break with John, we need to look at four texts. These are the texts that present his opinions about John. They are difficult texts, subtle but also violent. They are also as important for the future of Christianity as anything Jesus ever said.

(1) Already and Not Yet: Luke 5:33-38
(see also Matthew 9:15-17; Mark 2:18-22)

> They said to him, "The disciples of John fast often and offer prayers, . . . but yours eat and drink." Jesus said to them, "Can you make wedding guests fast while the bridegroom is with them? The days will come when the bridegroom is taken away from them, and then they will fast in those days."
>
> He told them a parable also, "No one tears a piece from a new garment and puts it upon an old garment; if he does, he will tear the new, and the piece from the new will not match the old. And no one puts new wine into old wineskins; if he does, the new wine will burst the skins and it will be spilled, and the skins will be destroyed. But new wine must be put into fresh wineskins."

Two ideas are at work here. The first is a practical distinction that exists between John's disciples and Jesus': John's disciples fast, Jesus' do not — although one day they will. This difference in the practice of fasting is caused by a different view of the future. John's disciples are ascetic in order to be ready for the judgment and the Messiah. "People get ready, there's a train a'comin'."

Christ's disciples, on the other hand, eat and drink like people in the world: like everybody else, in other words. In many ways, they live just like everybody else. This is because the one they long for is actually physically with them. One day he will go, he will leave. But his departure will not mean the end of the world (literally). It will mean only that they are without him now. At that point, *then,* they shall begin their wait. It will be fitting then for them to fast and expect. They will be without him, yes, but they will also be looking up, expecting the Last Day. Most Christians after Christ interpreted this text to refer to his second coming.

The important thing here for the history of ideas is that the time after Jesus leaves will be a time between: W. H. Auden's "for the time being."

There is a second, countervailing idea in the text. It is the concept that Christ's presence really does involve something new. "New wine must be put into fresh wineskins" (v. 38). The kingdom of God idea wrapped up in Jesus' preaching and teaching and in his timely presence is new. "If I drive out demons by the finger of God, then the kingdom of God has come to you" (Luke 11:20). The kingdom of God is substantially new. The old world cannot contain it. It changes everything it touches. The old structures of thought and existence are not adequate to hold it. They break when it is poured into them.

Thus two countervailing ideas are contained in the same passage. On the one hand, Christ is here, but not forever. When he leaves, there will come a "time being." At that time, pour on the vigilance! On the other hand, the kingdom is here, comparable to new wine. It is here in life but also different in essence from everything that has come before it.

The old cliché of New Testament scholarship that Jesus announced a kingdom that was "already and also not yet" present (i.e., *"schon"* and *"noch nicht"* in the language of the scholars who first emphasized this) is true. Jesus was different from John, who sounded one note. Jesus said: not yet, but soon.

The implications of Jesus' timing for anthropology, specifically for Christian anthropology, are important. The difference in timetable between Jesus of Nazareth and John the Baptist became the testtube, the heuristic crucible, in a most fruitful way for the Christian understanding of continuing sin and human nature in relation to the finality of God's revelation.

(2) Three Divisions in Time: Luke 16:16

> The law and the prophets were until John; since then the good news of the kingdom of God is preached, and everyone enters it violently.

This is a passage with which people who emphasize the continuity of Christ's message have got to make peace. It is discontinuous with everything that has gone before it. And it is hard to understand and even somewhat threatening. Specifically, the verb form "enters it violently" (βιάζεται) is troubling. Did Christ really say, "violently"?

Actually, the same basic idea structure found above, in Luke 5:33-38, is also present here in Luke 16:16. On the one hand, something new has come: "The law and the prophets were *until* John." John's entrance marks the end of the beginning, the beginning being the promise of fulfillment and fruition represented by the gift of the Law and the forward-looking predictions of the prophets who came after Moses. But that was then; this is now. John marked the end of that long line. He was definitely the last person in it.

But the not-yet of Christ's paradoxical model of the kingdom is just as present in this hammering verse as the "already," the "done." "Since then the good news of the kingdom of God is preached, and everyone enters it violently." This is a disturbed, disturbing time, the "since then," the time since John. The seed is being planted, the Word actively being voiced. There is an eruption of the kingdom of God that is also its expansion in the world.[1]

This idea is in the spirit of two other parables Christ told: Matthew 13:33, concerning the leaven in the flour; and Luke 13:18-19, concerning the mustard seed that became a tree. Something is actually happening, but it consists of breaking and entering. The kingdom of heaven is violent in the same way that the plant bursts through the soil when it grows. It uproots one's life in the place and context of one's inherited values and loyalties. It twists and bends as it also reshapes. It is not a process. It is not a slow burn. It is a ripping and a tearing, a re-formation. It is the contemporary work of God in lives and history.

What Luke 16:16 does, together with the other three texts that express Jesus' admiring measure of John, is to present a three-part division of time. The first part is the "biblical" phase, the period until John the Baptist. The biblical phase is represented by the Law and the prophets. The second part is the period of the kingdom's gouging through the husks and cover of the old world. This second phase or period is the time of the seed's development, the leaven's expansion, the time we ourselves live in: *schon* and *noch nicht*. The third frame is the coming of the Son of Man, what Christians call the second coming. This is the crushing total event that Jesus linked with the final judgment: the coming of the Son of Man in all his glory and his angels (Matthew 16:27; Mark 8:38; Luke 9:26; etc.).

Luke 16:16 and 5:33-38 portray a time line divided into three parts. John the Baptist's time line had only two parts. This difference, in its implications for the whole run of theology, is the beginning of Christianity's separation from Judaism.[2]

---

1. See Flusser's *Jesus,* 3rd edition (Jerusalem: The Magnes Press, 2001), p. 110.

2. A creative discussion of some implications of Jesus' separation from John over the eschatological timetable for the philosophy of history has been undertaken by David Pileggi, of Alexander College, Jerusalem, in an unpublished paper (1999) for Hebrew University entitled "The Place of History in Modern Jewish Thought." Pileggi's paper is a refutation of aspects of Amos Funkenstein's *Perceptions of Jewish History* (New York, 1993).

(3) The Time Being: Matthew 11:11-14

> Truly, I say to you, among those born of woman there has risen
> no one greater than John the Baptist; yet he who is least in the
> kingdom of heaven is greater than he. From the days of John the
> Baptist until now the kingdom of heaven has suffered violence
> and men of violence take it by force. For all the prophets and the
> law prophesied until John; and if you are willing to accept it, he
> is Elijah who is to come.

Although there is some conflation here,[3] there are also three new ideas
within this text concerning John in his relation to Jesus. These ideas are
in harmony with Luke 5:33-38 and 16:16.

The first idea is that John the Baptist was the greatest of all human
beings who ever lived before Jesus entered the scene. This is because
John summed up and in his summing up concluded the time of promise that goes back to the patriarchs and really back to primal man and
woman, Adam and Eve. John was God's *summation* of all that he had
ever done to save and bless his people.

The second idea is that any single person who is living now in the
kingdom of heaven is superior to John. This is a superlative statement.
It rules out development, evolution, and process. It means, rather, that
the speaker's message has created a new environment superior to all
that came before. This environment is the kingdom of heaven. It is identified with Jesus. We have here at least a two-part theory of historic time
in the kingdom of God. The first division is all time up to and including
John the Baptist, who was God's summation as well as his prelude. The
second division is the time since, the time of the kingdom of heaven.

The third idea, which occurs in v. 14, is that John is to Jesus what
Elijah is to the Messiah (Malachi 4:5): "[John] is Elijah who is to come."
The Messiah is present because John is his necessary immediate har-

---

3. "Conflation" is a term used by New Testament scholars specifically, and lit-
erary editors in general, to identify the mixing or co-mingling of different texts
into one single text.

binger. Thus Jesus is the Messiah. That is the unmistakable implication of Jesus' words.

This saying from Jesus has again altered the two-part chronology of John. For the Messiah is not the same as the "great and terrible day of the Lord." They are two different realities: (1) the Messiah preceding that day, and (2) the time of the kingdom of heaven, including many who are least. The inference, again, is of a present "time being."

In Christian theology, everything hangs on the time being.

(4) John and the New Age: Luke 7:24-28

> When the messengers of John had gone, he began to speak to the crowds concerning John: "What did you go out into the wilderness to behold? A reed shaken by the wind? What then did you go out to see? A man clothed in soft raiment? Behold, those who are gorgeously appareled and live in luxury are in kings' courts. What then did you go out to see? A prophet? Yes, I tell you, and more than a prophet. This is he of whom it is written, 'Behold, I send my messenger before thy face, who shall prepare thy way before thee' [Malachi 3:1]. I tell you, among those born of women, none is greater than John; yet he who is least in the kingdom of God is greater than he."

Two new ideas come out here, although each of them is parallel to ideas in the other three texts. The first idea is the explicit declaration that John the Baptist was a prophet of God. He was not a "reed shaken by the wind," the Vicar of Bray. Nor was he a TV evangelist, a "man clothed in soft raiment." In fact John came to inherit a king's house. But John's king's house proved to be a dungeon. So who was John? He was a prophet. His being "more than a prophet" refers to the fact that he was the last man in the queue, the "one-millionth customer" for whom the fireworks erupt and the brass band plays.

The second idea is the confirmation that John is "Elijah" or, rather, the Elijah figure. John is the immediate precursor of the Messiah. He points uniquely to the new age.

Nothing Comes from Nothing

As a boy, Isaac Newton is said to have observed an apple falling from a tree. This began a chain of reflections that led to his divining the principle of gravity. They tell you the exact same tree is still standing there in the garden of Woolsthorpe Manor, Lincolnshire, in the U.K.[4]

Quite late in his life, William Booth observed some alcoholics on the streets of London during his daily walk. He returned to his wife that afternoon, shut the door, and announced: "My dear, I have found my life's work."

Rod Serling backed into an idea, after winning three Emmy awards with very different material, for a network television show that was mysterious but not really supernatural, science fiction but somewhat tongue-in-cheek, scary but also ironic. He backed into it with a pilot entitled "Where Is Everybody?" The result? One hundred fifty-six episodes of *The Twilight Zone* that are now iconic and revered.

Where do big ideas come from, ideas with the power to bring change? How do we ever know that our idea is true enough, deep enough, subtle enough, or wide enough, to beget children "down to the third and fourth generation"?

The purpose of this book is to display the discontinuity of Jesus Christ in relation to his context. My interest is to stress again an old idea: that the historical Jesus really was the same Christ whom Christians love and adore. Would we have recognized in him then the One whom we adore now? My approach is historicist. It is interested in history, not any history and not history in every detail, but in one history that actually happened.

G. E. Lessing rejected historicism. Rudolf Bultmann rejected it, at least in his early influential work. E. P. Sanders rejected it, at least in his 1990 lecture at the University of London. They all said that you cannot ground the object of faith in a subject of history. History and faith are opposed. Christianity is a proposition of faith, not of empirical fact.

---

4. Another version of the story sets the tree in the garden of Trinity College, Cambridge.

Religion cannot be tied to facts, which are by nature extremely hard to verify, let alone interpret. Do we, can we, really know anything about what happened before we were born?

But Lessing, Bultmann, and Sanders, together with their students, were too skeptical! If we cannot surely say everything about Christ — John the Evangelist conceded the point unreservedly at the conclusion of his Gospel (21:25) — we can say something. Why be a Christian if we cannot? I would give up my religion in a minute if I became convinced that the one on whom I pin my hopes for "this life and the next" were a projected person.

Who is there in the world who will give his heart and whole self to a hope divorced from fact? What confidence could such a faith inspire? The truth is, faith divorced from fact does not exist — except in the case of spouses who are obtuse about their partners' adulteries, children who have no feel for what their parents are really like, and the characters in *The Glass Menagerie*. Fact-less Christians, unhistoricist believers, are persons in a Tennessee Williams play, feeding on illusion.

At the same time, it is *selbstverständlich* that we are considering a person who was born and lived within a context. He could not have emerged fully developed, for that would make him a figure of myth, an impossible being. No, he emerged from a context. And things catalyzed — his context, on one side, and his creativity, on the other — through his encounters with John the Baptist.

We can say that Jesus "hit upon" something in the three-part idea of salvation.

Here is the progress of the idea: If Christ brought something substantially or essentially new to the world, then everyone after him would be breathing the air of his newness. The thing Christ brought is the kingdom of God. The kingdom was characterized for Jesus by a vibrant concept of mutual love, which extended the second great commandment of the Law (Leviticus 19:18) to one's enemies; by a fervent and ideologically driven active association with lawbreakers and unclean people, something Jesus more or less "stumbled on" as a result of the three-part eschatology he developed in relation to John; and a pulling back from imminence, a resistance to temporal urgency. This was because God alone, not Jesus or any human being, knew the date of the end (Acts 1:7).

The kingdom of God had come with Christ's ministry (Matthew 4:17) but had not come in completion. Completion would come, but it would not come tomorrow. The end was beyond tomorrow.

The consequence of Christ's open-ended chronology was, over time, *a "both-and" understanding of the human situation*. It was a both-and in the present, anchored within an either-or from the standpoint of the past and also from the standpoint of the future. This is to say, the follower of Christ exists within a present in which the new has arrived. Jesus himself is the new in person. But after he leaves, there is a period, without cap or seal, in which the new and the old coexist. The follower of Christ exists with one foot in the old and one in the new. Or you could say that the Christian exists with both feet in the old and at the same time both feet in the new.

All approaches of men and women to the disturbing question of the world's potential improvement are related to this model. If I live only in the period of the "Law and the prophets," I can never get to where I want to be going within the category of hope or dream or desire. If I live in the past, even if it is a past of promise, I will never see the last day. "How long, O Lord, how long?"

If I live in the time of fulfillment — that is, if I think that all was fulfilled in Christ's arrival, his first advent, to use the old language — then I will look for and expect victory and blessing on every front. Yet disappointment will invariably come. I shall lose my hope of victory and of the triumph of the good.

But if I live in the time *between,* in the second of the three compartments of human narrative, then I am living in two worlds simultaneously. I can work toward "the dream," my dream, but will not feel God-forsaken when the dream is never fully or even partly achieved. I can live with the plural loose ends of my experience of living, yet not be satisfied with them, desperate over them, cynical about them, hopeless because of them, a nihilist in the acceptance of them.

Jesus' concept of time was not acute. Nor was it a form of our modern expression, "Whatever." Finality would arrive, but not yet (Matthew 13:24-30). Human beings live in the middle ages.

David Flusser, who was neither a systematic theologian nor a Christian, understood Christ's discontinuity when he wrote, "Jesus is the only known thinker who drew from this scheme the logical conclusion that until the final destruction of the wicked, the righteous and the sinners would necessarily coexist" (p. 263).

The Birth of Christian Compassion

When I say to traditional Christians that the origin of the classic Reformation approach to continuing sin and struggle within the Christian life is in Jesus' eschatology, their eyes glaze over. I lose them. What they tell me is that they see the origin of Christianity's tender approach to human sin and infirmity in the compassion of Jesus acted out in such stories as the "woman who was a sinner" who anointed his feet (Luke 7:36-50; cf. Matthew 26:6-13 and Mark 14:3-9); the children whom he took in his arms (Mark 10:13-16); and the centurion whose servant was at "the point of death" (Luke 7:1-10; Matthew 8:5-13). Jesus' world-shaking Christian love came from the way he was.

My response to that as a theologian is this: But where did Jesus' compassion come *from?* What *caused* it? What birthed it? What ideas engendered it? For nothing comes from nothing.

Nothing comes into being unconditioned. God is unconditioned. But nothing exists in the physical historic world that is not conditioned. Jesus' compassion came from somewhere. If it were just there, *tout fait,* then he was not a human being. Nothing human and created is ever just there. It is formed and informed, shaped and influenced.

What I am saying is a form of Käsemann's once-famous dictum: "Apocalyptic was the mother of all Christian theology."[5] Käsemann wrote that sentence in connection with St. Paul, but it is applicable to

---

5. "See the Beginnings of Christian Theology," in *New Testament Questions of Today* (London: SCM, 1969), p. 102.

the whole of New Testament thought. Christ's three-part eschatology is able to explain the compassionate approach to people that marked so many of his interactions. Christ's three-part eschatology is the womb in thought for the birth of Christian compassion.

Compassion comes from understanding and sympathy. The understanding implicit in Christ's three-part eschatology is a window into men and women. Human existence is theological in that we have become acquainted with the new and are responding to it. In our salvation, or commitment or new birth or conversion or just the impulse to open up to divine grace — however one may wish to say it — we exist in the new. *But we also exist in the old.* This is because the new is not yet all around us. Jesus is the new in person, yet the world as a whole still suffers under the spell of the old. It is cold out there. The hold effected by death, the world, and the flesh, by the devil, the law, and sin — the two "trinities" of universal racial captivity — is unyielding. Yet we are new and live in the confidence that the hold of the old has been broken at the root. The veins and human delivery systems for nutrient within the massive enfolding thicket and wasteland of the human world have been cut off in such a way that the sin will one day be completely atrophied.

The ground for Jesus' compassion was his theology of the end-time. The threat of the Law, the threat of God's impending, oncoming, and non-exception-granting righteousness, was John the Baptist's great theme. It was unbearable unless conceived in immediate collision with the erupting end. But the threat of the cathartic end *relaxed* in the way of Christ, as he was the beginning of the end but not the end, just as John the Baptist was, and also triggered, the end of the beginning.

Human nature under threat but not under immediate threat, the person in the inner confidence of the new yet also in the outward reality of "same old, same old" — that is the starting point and also the center of the Christian view of humanity's precarious existence on the planet. It allows each actor in the drama of being human to survive in hope and make a way forward in reality. It allows space for compassion to be expressed and lived out, the compassion of God to human and the compassion of human to human.

Simul iustus et peccator

Jesus anticipated in his eschatologically motivated approach to weakened faltering people what Christian theology understands by the phrase *simul iustus et peccator.* This phrase originated with the Protestant Reformation. It means, "loved and at the same time fully human." *Iustus* means "justified" or in harmony with God, loved by God unconditionally. *Peccator* means "sinner," one whose sin cannot be synchronized or reconciled with God and God's perfection. *Peccator* defines the human being whose nature consists in original sin evenly distributed.

What Martin Luther intended by the phrase *simul iustus et peccator* was a way of expressing what he read in St. Paul, who in one breath addressed his readers as blood-bought, Spirit-filled, newborn people in the new age of Christ, then turned right around and told them they had deserted Christ, mishandled the gospel, and brought on themselves God's curse.

Luther was helped immensely by his discovery that the original addressees of Paul's letters were regarded both as brothers and sisters in the band *and* as falling, fallen persons: "To the church of God which is at Corinth, to those sanctified in Christ Jesus, called to be saints. . . . I hear there is fornication among you" (1 Corinthians 1:2 and 5:1). Paul's dynamic of address, which combined the indicative (you are yoked as saints to God) with the imperative (change your lives for they are in an appalling mess) impressed Luther. For Luther, this became the key to living as a Christian in the real, broken world.

On the one hand, Luther's anthropology saw the sick world as loved and even affirmed by God's grace, as in "Neither do I condemn thee" (John 8:11a). On the other hand, his anthropology envisaged the divinely esteemed world as caught on the hook of unbending divine demand, as in "Go and sin no more" (8:11b).

Here we are at the intersection of the historical Jesus' continuity and his discontinuity. The discontinuity is Jesus' riveting message of a new world in relation to an old retired world. The birthing in the world of Christian compassion as the result of a relaxed apocalyptic is its discontinuity. But this may not be exactly what traditional Christians wish it were. That is because it came from something. It is a big idea that came from a specific insight.

Jesus' time frame, his open-ended and transitional apocalyptic, combined hope for the new and acceptance of the old in a truly original way. It allowed for a distinctive "mixed" approach to human beings, which looks to us like Christian compassion. We read Christ's compassion as if it were the fully developed item. It was not. Grace is not the romantic or sentimental projection of a wish. It is also not intuitive, or normal, to human beings. Judgment and contempt and implacability are much more firmly rooted human reactions to the world's ambiguity. Compassion is what we want. Compassion is what we seldom get, either from the world or in the world.

Christ's tri-focal view of man and woman in their relation to God's final judgment opened a space in which the human being could stand. This is the continuity of Jesus with Christianity. It is the continuity of Jesus' strange futurism with Christian compassion as we know it. There is therefore no more fruitful a *discontinuity* in the history of theology than the discontinuity of timing that separated John, the prophet of God, from his even greater follower.

Jesus the Christian

*Jesus was primarily the "Evangelist" (without qualification),
so far as that can be said before Easter.*

ERNST KÄSEMANN

If all time can be divided into three parts, on Christ's model, then
Christian disciples find themselves standing in the second act of the
drama. This sets the scene for a compassionate outlook on human experience. It stimulates compassion for human beings.

But there is a further, arresting newness in the words and acts recorded of the man. This chapter presents that newness.

Five areas or themes mark out the newness of Christ's ministry.
Each of these is discontinuous by definition with what has gone before. The five themes are his inaugural message of repentance (Matthew 4:17); the annunciatory exorcisms (Luke 11:20); the "antitheses" of
Matthew 5:21-47, by which a new Moses is declared; the teaching on purity (Mark 7:1-23 and Matthew 15:1-20); and the association with sinners
(Matthew 9:11; Mark 2:15-17; and Luke 5:29-32). These five themes together represent the discontinuity of Jesus the Christian.

Repentance as Possibility: Matthew 4:17

From that time Jesus began to preach, saying,
"Repent, for the kingdom of heaven is at hand."

The context of Christ's opening salvo is important. His announcement follows from the news that John has been arrested (Matthew 4:12). The ministry of John being over in material terms, the age of the Law and the prophets having come to its end, now the "time being," the second stage of the plan, has begun.

There are two fundamental ideas represented in this text. The first idea is more important for the history of Christianity than the second. But the second is the basis for the first. Christ's message of repentance came out of a prior idea, the three-stage eschatology that distinguished his thinking from John the Baptist. Just as the Christian idea of compassion grew from the context of the mix of sinners and the righteous in the between-time of God's kingdom on earth, so did the Christian concept of repentance.

You cannot invite people to repent, which is to say "I am sorry," in the context of imminent judgment. Why? Because there is no time! It is just that straightforward. You need time to repent. You need time to be sorry, to say you are sorry, to list and know what you are sorry for, and to communicate the fact that you are sorry, especially to those whom you have sinned against.

The principle is the same in relation to death. There has to be time, just a little bit of time, for a dying man to "come to himself" (Luke 15:17). Sometimes in ministry I have seen a person's personal time run out. We term this an "untimely death." The end came — the personal eschatology — through a car wreck, a cardiac arrest, or a blood vessel burst in the brain.

Or I see it in the eyes of a person with a feeding tube. Her eyes tell you, "I have something more to say. Please get a piece of paper so I can try to write down the words, 'I love you' or 'Forgive me.'" I see it in the face of the son who does not get there in time to say goodbye to his father. It is too late. He got there too late.

Nothing is worse and more costly for human peace of mind than running out of time when there is still something to say.

That is why Christ says, "Repent," and is able to mean it. John the Baptist had thrown the book at his hearers. They needed to speed up their restitutions and their reparations. "Even now the axe is laid to the root of the tree." John had even used language similar to Jesus' to announce his mission (Matthew 3:2). But what disillusionment for John when the deterrent of which he spoke did not arrive, when the chaff was not burned, through Christ, with unquenchable fire. By way of contrast, Jesus' concept of time, of God's wrapping up of time, was open-ended and transitional. Open-endedness gives a person the possibility and chance of saying "I am sorry" clearly, forcefully, and with the possibility, at least, of a new creation.

This is why Ebenezer Scrooge is overjoyed at the very end of *A Christmas Carol*. At the end of his long night of inexpressibly painful encounter with himself, Scrooge realizes he still has time. It is *still* Christmas Day. It is not too late to make restitution. Scrooge's repentance turns on the time he is given, even if it is short: time first to speak it, then to love (Tiny Tim) and act on his love, and finally to become, over time, the man he was meant to be. Repentance requires time. Even if it is just two seconds — the time to say "I'm sorry" and be heard — repentance requires time.

Since the kingdom of heaven is interim in Jesus' view, his call to repentance is a real thing. It can take place. The repentance he orders is possible.

But what is it exactly? What constitutes repentance? And what is the newness of its essence?

Here we have to enter into dialogue with what Christianity later became. In order to understand the idea in *nuce,* that is, what Jesus was expressing in its original context, we have to argue back from the idea as it later grew and expanded. We have to compare repentance under the New Covenant, theologically understood, with repentance under the Old Covenant, theologically understood.

The Law of Moses, without Christ, holds the world accountable and everyone in it (Romans 3:19). But the Law offers no solution to guilt save precise parity. Repentance under the Law means restitution, the *lex talionis,* which is satisfactory and acceptable when accompanied by sincere repugnance toward the sin committed. But the "Law and the prophets," the entire age before John that also culminated in his blunt message, does not possess the depth of the later Christian insight of original sin.

Original sin refers to the universal, indelible, intrinsic character of human egotism. In Christianity, specifically in Pauline Christianity, original sin typifies all human nature and therefore all personified human natures, that is, individual people. So repentance that is tied to equivalency — the punishment fits the crime — is not adequate. This is because punishment in Christianity is for who we are, as original sinners, not just for what we have done, our actual sins. Repentance by means of equivalent restitution does not, cannot, quench the fire of God. That is why Paul said that "the righteousness of God has been manifested apart from Law" (Romans 3:21). It had to be manifested other than by Law, since "no human being" — no original sinner — "will be justified in God's sight by works of the Law" (Romans 3:20).

Paul penetrated straight to the heart of an idea implicit in Jesus' actual historic Galilean call to repentance — that the Law and the prophets were not able to provide the escape route for humans under judgment. Jesus' inaugural summons as delivered in Mark's Gospel helps the idea implicit in our text, Matthew 4:17, to be just a little plainer. The Markan long form reads this way: "The time is fulfilled, and the kingdom of God is at hand; repent, and believe in the gospel" (1:15). The gospel represents the new age, a time for an escape route unknown to John.

Jesus' portrait of human nature is filled out significantly in his teachings concerning purity, discussed below, and in his association with sinners, also discussed below. His view of human nature's true depth and interior reality, together with his implication that only those who acknowledge the moral paralysis resulting from the conflict present in all people between the outward and the inward can make any headway against it, transformed the idea and experience of repentance into something completely different from what it had been under the

Law and the prophets. Repentance for Jesus was completely different from repentance for John.

To measure the discontinuity of Christ's words, you have to measure their discontinuity in effect, their centrifugal force. You have to work backwards. It is a point of method. Arresting yet enigmatic on their own terms in their immediate context, his words had an effect. They were leaven. From his three-part scheme of salvation, Jesus' idea of the future immediately brought into being, within the ethical sphere, a view of repentance that was open-ended rather than weighted according to the offense. Repentance is for the whole person! Nothing he or she does can compensate for the total problem represented to God by the human being. The human being is 100 percent out of harmony with the righteous God. This man, this woman cannot repent by means of an action. He or she is required, rather, *to be sorry for his or her very existence.* So strong is the demand of the Law when it penetrates to the extensive subterranean "lower depths" (Gorky) of the universal human nature that death is required rather than the small change of moral endeavor.

We have to read *back,* then, from the centrifugal implications in the New Testament that were carried within Christ's initial summons: "Repent, for the kingdom of heaven is at hand." What is the discontinuity of Matthew 4:17 in its original context? It is the enabling of repentance to take place in the context of grace, grace meaning a *period of grace.* The attack made inherent in the divine demand is restrained by the existence of a time between. The interim assumed in the preaching of Christ is the *novum.* It offers what people today call "a little space."

The observation I am making is that the famously discovered eschatology of Jesus of Nazareth is not the rock of offense that stands in the way of integrating traditional Christianity with the historical Jesus. That is what Wrede, Weiss, and Schweitzer believed. They saw Christ's eschatology as an offense, unassimilable to modern humankind and to traditional Christianity. They could not pass beyond the barrier it represented to them.

They failed to see its positive, *Christian* impact. Christ's eschatology was the enabling word for the concept of grace, in antithesis to Law, which is the essence of Christian experience and teaching. This is why Käsemann felt able to refer to Jesus as "the Evangelist (without qualification)." The second phase of the plan, according to Jesus, gives time and place to the profound subjective appalledness at human nature's paralysis that is repentance. The time being, the time at hand, is the enabling word for what Christians term the gospel.

The discontinuity of Matthew 4:17 with John the Baptist's acute timetable is the seedbed for the possibility of human conversion. It is also the germ of St. Paul's understanding that saints and sinners coexist in the present tense within the family of faith. It is thus directly the origin of Luther's magnificent inference that the righteous and the unrighteous coexist within the psychology of every individual. Like the mixed family of God within the new transitional aeon, the individual Christian heart is also divided equally between *iustus* and *peccator*.

Exorcisms in the Time Being: Luke 11:20

"If it is by the finger of God that I cast out demons, then the kingdom of God has come upon you."

The exorcisms of Christ have rarely been regarded as an invention. The usual interpretation in the literature has been that his exorcisms, the casting out of demons, were an expected mark of a traveling teacher, not only in the late Hellenistic world of Greco-Roman antiquity but also in the Jewish context of the later Second Temple period. *Thaumaturgy* was more or less expected in wide circles of the Gentile world. It was also a confirming sign of a rabbi who was close to God.

Formally, exorcism was a ministry almost universally awaited of holy men. Materially, exorcism was probably a wise handling of mental illness within a credulous projecting culture.

The weight of this saying in Luke 11:20, which is Christ's interpretation of what he was doing through his exorcisms, relates directly to the issue of discontinuity versus continuity. It relates to the question of the proportions of discontinuity and continuity to be found within his message. The question runs in two directions: On the one hand, to what extent was Jesus' message discontinuous with what had gone before (i.e., Second Temple Judaism and the context of John the Baptist) and to what extent was it continuous with it? On the other hand, to what extent was the message discontinuous with what came later (i.e., Christianity as, for example, developed by Paul) and to what extent was it continuous with that?

The third quest for the historical Jesus underlines the continuity of Christ with his Jewish context and his discontinuity with classical Christianity. I seek to stress the continuity of the historical Jesus with classical Christianity and his discontinuity with Judaism. The issue oscillates in the history of theology, depending on fashion and historical trends. But I do not see how one can account for the Christian movement, in its centrifugal motion toward the universal, without reference to the canonical message of Christ. Notwithstanding the force and effects of fashion in scholarship and theology, and notwithstanding the self-evident influence on Jesus of Judaism, which was his heritage, the drift of history is on the side of Jesus' "Christianity."

If the seeds of Christianity's concept of grace are not located within the deep stratum of Jesus tradition, then the burden of Christianity's founding and derivation has to be carried by Paul. That is an old alternative in the scholarship. But it is an unreasonable one.[1] It makes Paul into a "religious genius" way beyond his own self-understanding and statements about himself. It makes Paul in relation to Christianity what Joseph Smith became in relation to Mormonism. Why shunt the burden over to Paul when the direction of several provocative texts from Jesus is toward a theology of grace?

Jesus' exorcisms, whatever they may have looked like or consisted in as they "really were," were a demonstration to him that "the kingdom of God has come upon you." A reference exists here to Exodus 8:19: "And the magicians said to Pharaoh, 'This is the finger of God.'" A second Exodus is in mind: a new deliverance has come to Israel. It is a

---

1. See David Wenham's *Paul: Follower of Jesus or Founder of Christianity?* (Grand Rapids: Eerdmans, 1995).

deliverance both present and future, for the "Son of man will come at an hour you do not expect" (Matthew 24:44). Its open-ended character is everything.

The number of exorcisms reported of Jesus in the Gospels points to their rock-solid place in the tradition. They confirmed and were an eschatological sign of the palpability of the kingdom of heaven. Because of the very presence and substance of Jesus' ministry, even if only for a period of three years or less, the scheme is so much less acute than the pitch sounded by John. The relaxation of the urgency, tied to the physical presence of the messenger Jesus, confirmed by the "finger of God" through him against the demons of the world, opened a window. This window opened onto Christianity.

The "Antitheses": Matthew 5:21-22, 27-28, 43-45

"You have heard that it was said to the men of old, 'You shall not kill; and whoever kills shall be liable to judgment.' But I say to you that every one who is angry with his brother shall be liable to judgment; and whoever insults his brother shall be liable to the council, and whoever says, 'You fool!' shall be liable to the hell of fire. . . .

"You have heard that it was said, 'You shall not commit adultery.' But I say to you that every one who looks at a woman lustfully has already committed adultery with her in his heart. . . .

"It was also said, 'Whoever divorces his wife, let him give her a certificate of divorce.' But I say to you that every one who divorces his wife, except on the ground of unchastity, makes her an adulteress; and whoever marries a divorced woman commits adultery. . . .

"You have heard that it was said, 'You shall love your neighbor and hate your enemy.' But I say to you, love your enemies and pray for those who persecute you, so that you may be sons of your Father who is in heaven; for he makes his sun rise on the evil and on the good, and sends rain on the just and on the unjust."

These are the first, second, third, and sixth "antitheses," as they are usually known, from the Sermon on the Mount. They are new by definition, because Jesus contrasts *his* (re-)statements of certain principles of the Law with those deriving from *Moses*. The contrast takes the rhetorical form: "You have heard that it was said to the men of old . . . , but I say to you. . . ." This manner of speaking is antithetical. Two ideas are compared not as enlargements or enhancements or with changed emphases, but rather as contradictory. The second statement, from Christ, supplants the first statement, from "Moses." If *supplanting* seems too strong a verb, then *deepening* may be better, but with the meaning of going to the heart of the matter so vigorously that the new idea is completely different from the old.

Christ's deepening of the old idea is similar in effect to 2 Corinthians 3:7-10, where Paul compares the New Covenant with the Old. Paul says that the new dispensation of the Spirit of Christ is brighter than the old dispensation of condemnation (i.e., from Mount Sinai and the Law). But it is an antithesis rather than a difference in quality or extent, because "what once had splendor has come to have no splendor at all, because of the splendor that surpasses it" (v. 10). The new outshines the old to the point of extinction, or at least extinction from the observer's point of view.

The antitheses of Jesus are framed in rhetorical terms of discontinuity rather than continuity. The set-up negates the old. There is no development or evolution here. There is instead decontextualization. The old prescriptions of the Law are being rewritten, radically. You could say that Christ is arguing back to the root of the Law's demand. He is getting down to its intended essence. Christ's radical redefinition is conservative in that it returns to first principles, to what God intended originally through the proscription. But the format is a contrasting one, expressed in extreme terms. The practice of the new "law" will be entirely different from the practice of the old.

The First Antithesis: Murder in Relation to Anger

As always in the treatment of discontinuity and continuity within the historical Jesus' statements, there is something in the formal fact of announciation that affects the material content of the ethic. The idea of a *novum* creates in itself content that is materially new.

The *novum* of the first antithesis consists materially in the extent of the wrong that is proscribed. Murder is subject to judgment. But the root of murder, which is anger, is also singled out for judgment. Thus the angry person is in danger of hell as much as the capital murderer is. The distinction between the outward act and the inward impelling thought is erased. This is revolutionary, as every reader of it in the history of Christianity has immediately understood. It equalizes intention and action. It puts motive and consequence on a par.

This is the opposite of casuistry. It is the opposite of the standard gambit offered in standard psychotherapy, by which the counselor comforts the conscience of the patient by saying, "There is nothing unusual about the *thought* you had. It's just bad if you acted on it. Did you?" "Well, no, not exactly." "All right, then. See! You are being too hard on yourself."

Human defense systems love this classic casuistical distinction — which exists in all cultures from Second Temple Judaism to the Jesuit order to psychotherapists who counsel people today — between the deed and the thought. Ironically, and I speak from three decades in parish ministry, there are a lot more "acts" out there than you might think at first. Persons who say, "I am not a bad person. I've never actually broken one of the Ten Commandments," are usually deceiving themselves. Many more people have appeared in court than you might at first believe.

The point is, the focus of the first antithesis upon the thought rather than the deed is arduous and upsetting. It is simply so emphatic. Moreover, the thought, or insult, merits hell (v. 22)! There is no hierarchy of sins offered here. The doing is not worse than the thinking. Both are equally culpable. Both deserve the judgment of God.

That a dynamic view of human personality is understood in the first antithesis is obvious. This is a material difference from the Law of Moses, which is focused on the overt. The inward factor of human guilt that is in play here is the beginning of the Christian theory, or doctrine rather, of original sin. Jesus stressed elsewhere the interior facts in behavior, as, for example, when he described the scribes and Pharisees as whitewashed sepulchers that appear outwardly clean and white but are filled inside with dead men's bones (Matthew 23:27). The inner side of immoral actions is nowhere better stated in the Jesus tradition than here. And it is yoked to discontinuity.

The immediate discontinuity is with the Baptist's prescriptive ethic rooted in his two-stage picture of the world. Little or no reflection is possible when the ax is laid to the root of the tree. "Stop it! Stop it this instant, or I will blow your head off!"

That would be like the shocking scene toward the beginning of the classic western film *The Searchers* (1956), John Ford's analysis of racism and vengeance and also of sacrificial love. The settlers' sod-house is surprised suddenly by Indians intent on massacre. No one is there — the men have all been tricked to go elsewhere — except one man together with his wife and three children. They are completely exposed and completely vulnerable. Suddenly, by the flight of some startled birds, the little family realizes they are surrounded, doomed to die, or be raped and die. The teenaged daughter screams, and her mother cuts the scream short with a slap. It is a terrible, shocking moment in movie history. Acute eschatology: no time for words of comfort or regret. The character of John the Baptist's overwhelming verbal attack is the same. No quarter is possible.

Jesus of Nazareth is speaking in the moment of reflection and possible repentance. Yet the time is coming. The old Moses is superannuated. The new, "I say unto you," is radical, going to the root of the tree. But the tree contains concentric rings of time and growth. The tree has layers created through the passage of time. In the already-but-not-yet of Jesus' presence with the people, there consists a real and not illusory *pause*. It is a profound pause, by which his anthropology is formed in the way of depth.

The Christian idea of original sin is born in the first antithesis. It is given words in the "time being" of one dissident thinker's delayed apocalyptic.

The Second Antithesis: Adultery in Relation to Lust

Jesus' saying about adultery of the heart strengthens the first antithesis. It is a vivid restatement of the same principle of integrated human behavior. The action of adultery is no more culpable than its thought or fantasy. Its gestating inner fantasy is no less guilty than its flagrant acting out.

The second antithesis makes explicit a connection that is implicit in the first. Not only is lust equivalent to adultery, as insult is equivalent to murder (v. 22), but the thought holds within itself the completion of the act. The thought is not just the seed: it is the fully developed tree. "I say to you that everyone who looks at a woman lustfully has already committed adultery" (v. 28). Desire and implementation are the same thing!

This amounts to an extremely irritating increase in the volume of the wrath faced by the person in final perspective. "Nowhere to run, nowhere to hide." Significantly, the volume here, the heat, is much greater than John the Baptist's. Since John's acutely short time frame did not allow for nuance, layeredness, or reflection, the spotlight was on chargeable guilty crimes, such as avarice, extortion, hoarding, bribery, rape, robbery, and envy (Luke 3:10-14). John thought those crimes were susceptible to correction. They could be given up.

Jesus' supposition concerning the end allows for depth and analysis. But his indictment is worse than John's ever was. There is not one man who has ever lived — the single exception being Christ himself — who is not an adulterer under the terms of the second antithesis. Jesus' relaxation of John's urgency commits him to an anthropology that is much more worrisome. The *unconscious* life of the human race is the beast, for who can control his or her fantasies? The "1-900- numbers" of sex and greed are always ringing. Therefore under the Law of Moses, expanded now ten thousand times in scope by Christ the "new Moses" *(Moses mosissime),* the human race in its entirety should be stoned. The continuity is obvious with St. Paul's anthropology from Romans 3:10-12, which is itself an interpretation of Psalms 14 and 53. "No one is righteous, no, not one; no one understands, no one seeks for God. All have turned aside, together they have gone wrong, no one does good, not even one."

Christ's second antithesis strengthens the first by repetition, or rather by application of the principle of inwardness to the area of the sexual id. The second antithesis equates the impulse with the commission. The impulse actually equals the commission. And the second antithesis makes the divine wrath into an attitude with regard to the anthropology and essence of being human rather than its symptoms. Adultery, like anger, is ontology. It is psycho-genetic.

It is not anachronistic to say this, for "psycho-genetic" means inherited. The drive to sexual fantasy is inherited. It is normal in that it comes with the compound package of human existence. God is thus against the whole "normal" identity of human beings, which Christian theology terms original sin. God is not against us for what we do. He is against us for who we are.

Thus Jesus' comparatively relaxed eschatology produces a terrible indictment that requires a savior and an atonement. Luther understood the Sermon on the Mount not as prescriptive or even as prescriptive in an interim way. Luther understood the Sermon on the Mount as descriptive. The first and second antitheses are a most alarming description. "Wretched man that I am! Who will deliver me from this body of death?" (Romans 7:24). The first and second antitheses are the Proto-Evangelium in the recollected words of the historical Jesus.

The Third Antithesis: No Divorce

This book is a study in New Testament theology. It seeks to represent Jesus of Nazareth "as he really was" and at the same time to reflect on the origins of Christian theology. It seeks to understand historically the connection between the founder and the movement he founded. The connection is an organic one.

Christian insights such as original sin, which is the anthropology of the religion, and the relation between savedness *(iustus)* and persisting humanness *(peccator)* are developments from the Jesus tradition. They are rooted concretely in a difference in eschatology between Jesus and John the Baptist. The interim status of the time of Jesus, the kingdom of heaven on earth, which is the distance between the end of the Law and the prophets that was signified by John's ministry, on the one hand, and the final advent of the Son of Man, the judgment to come, on the other, creates a space for diagnosis, analysis, assessment. The interim status of the time of Jesus creates a period of depth, repentance by the whole person, complete self-assessment in the light of the end-time. The third antithesis of the Sermon on the Mount construes the wrath of God in the most exceptionless and most anti-casuistical manner in the whole body of Christ's sayings. The third antithesis forbids divorce.

Luke 16:18 probably gives the original form of the third antithesis of Matthew 5:32: "Every one who divorces his wife and marries another commits adultery, and he who marries a woman divorced from her husband commits adultery." The Luke form is probably prior, because the Matthew version inserts a qualification: "except on the grounds of unchastity."

The tendency of the original antithesis is absolutist. While Jewish law allowed women a small safeguard if their husbands divorced them, that safeguard being a legal certificate given at the end of a sort of due process, the Law of Moses assumed the fact of divorce. We could say that the Law of Moses recognized an inevitable fact of life, yet insisted on some protection for the victim.

Jesus' antithesis to that old former acquiescence was to rule out divorce altogether: divorce is not allowed because it creates adultery. The new "law" allows no room for extenuating circumstances or special cases. It is awesomely thorough. The third antithesis of Christ is almost universally regarded by scholars, even the most skeptical scholars, as authentic. It is true to Christ's actual words. This lack of skepticism regarding the saying is founded on its extremism. Rabbinic thought of the Second Temple was on the whole reasonable, compassionate, open to the extraordinary or unusual circumstance, and usually allowing for the existence of competing values or goods that might affect the implementation of a given law. The Law of Moses was humane.

Jesus shows none of that here. His law is exceptionless and therefore rooted in the divine command absolutely. There is a straight verticality to the third antithesis that can be explained only if it is understood, if it was spoken, as Word and revelation.

I understand the third antithesis as a directive arising from the first and second antitheses. The law of Christ assaults the whole man, the whole woman. It is an attack on identity, not on the symptoms and actions that spring from identity. The law of Christ flattens the angry as well as the angry murderers, the lustful as well as the lustful fornicators. The law, in other words, as homogenized by the new Moses, is total war on normal human existence and experience. Now this law is applied to marriage. Human frailty is blocked. It is not "understood."

The irony in the theology of Christ's law is that it is born from a less urgent dread of the last day, yet grows into a more intimidating discussion of the problem of being human. John's ax to the root of the tree is a slap in the face. It engenders panic. Jesus' apocalyptic is a stay of execution that requires a more powerful medicine.

The antitheses of the Sermon on the Mount are all preface to Matthew 5:48: "Ye, therefore, must be perfect, as your heavenly Father is perfect."

The Sixth Antithesis: Loving the Enemy

This is the command to love your enemies. Like the other antitheses, it comes from the eschatology of Christ. It is a stunning case of a theological deduction.

This is the logic: the "Father . . . makes his sun rise on the evil and on the good, and sends rain on the just and on the unjust" (Matthew 5:45). This is the interim fact of the wrath: it holds off. The "good" and the "bad" are mixed up together until the day of the Lord (Matthew 13:47-50). Until then, no one knows who is the justified and who is the sinner.

It is like Kierkegaard's knight of faith.[2] He is anonymous because we cannot know who he is exactly. His good works are quiet and unself-conscious; therefore they are seldom observed as such by the world. It is hard to distinguish between the knight of faith and the rest of the world. In the same way, the righteous and the sinners are all mixed up into one, "for he sends his rain on the just and the unjust." This means we have to love them all. We have to love all human beings, the unjust as well as the just. Why? Because we do not know who specifically they are.

Here we need to turn on its head an old maxim in theology: If all cats are gray in the dark, then how can we make distinctions among them? The maxim is told in criticism of the Augustinian/Lutheran idea of original sin. If *all* men and women are sinners, then why do anything to resist obvious sin in the world and thus try to make the world a better place? If there are no distinctions in *being,* then why make distinctions in *acting?* The point may be apt, in one sphere, but in Jesus' saying it is another thing altogether. All human beings live in the same world. God rules over that world (i.e., the sun and the rain of v. 45). If God relates to all human beings providentially, then we have to relate to them all providentially, and gracefully, too. This is because if we hate our enemy, we may be mistaken: the person we thought was our enemy may turn out to have been our neighbor. We have to love everybody. And if we have to love everybody, we have to love those who are, or who appear to be, our enemies also.

The sixth antithesis simply says that our enemies are a subset of everybody. Since we have got to love everybody so as to miss nobody, then we have to love our enemies in particular. This is the origin, from the between-time of Christ, of the command to love one's enemies. Christian compassion, or better, the birth of Christian compassion in the world of ideas and experience, is not arbitrary. It did not just happen. Nothing comes from nothing. Rather, Christian compassion came from the logic of human mixedness in the period from John the Baptist to the (second) coming of the Son of Man.

2. In SK's *Fear and Trembling* (Princeton: Princeton University Press, 1983).

True compassion, which is grace to the unlovable and undeserving, is the great effective change agent in human history, collective and individual. But this was not clearly understood before the emergence of Christianity. Several religions have taught charity and alms to the poor and unfortunate. Almost all societies have, even in ancient times, made allowances for the failing and the handicapped, the blind and the lame, both in body and mind. But the specific word to love your enemies *as such* was new with Christ. Was it a discovery? Like everything else in life, it had a point of origin. The point of origin was the observation that until the sun comes up, until the ultimate and ultimately discerning day of the Lord dawns, "all cats are gray." All human beings look alike to the unwise, the imperceptive eye of the beholder, until the divine wisdom separates the good from the bad. God will do that. We ourselves cannot. So love the whole race. The direct inference of this is to love your enemies. This is the origin of Christian charity in the words of the historical Jesus.

Purity Control: Mark 7:1-8, 14-23 (cf. Matthew 15:1-20)

Now when the Pharisees gathered together to him, with some of the scribes, who had come from Jerusalem, they saw that some of his disciples ate with hands defiled, that is, unwashed. (For the Pharisees, and all the Jews, do not eat unless they wash their hands, observing the tradition of the elders; and when they come from the market place, they do not eat unless they purify themselves; and there are many other traditions which they observe, the washing of cups and pots and vessels of bronze.) And the Pharisees and the scribes asked him, "Why do your disciples not live according to the tradition of the elders, but eat with hands defiled?" And he said to them, "Well did Isaiah prophesy of you hypocrites, as it is written, 'This people honors me with their lips, but their heart is far from me; in vain do they worship me, teaching as doctrine the precepts of men' [Isaiah 29:13]. You leave the commandment of God, and hold fast the tradition of men." . . .

And he called the people to him again, and said to them, "Hear me, all of you, and understand: There is nothing outside a man which by going into him can defile him; but the things which come out of a man are what defile him." And when he had entered the house, and left the people, his disciples asked him about the parable. And he said to them, "Then are you also without understanding? Do you not see that whatever goes into a man from outside cannot defile him, since it enters, not his heart but his stomach, and so passes on?" . . . And he said, "What comes out of a man is what defiles a man. For from within, out of the heart of man come evil thoughts, fornication, theft, murder, adultery, coveting, wickedness, deceit, licentiousness, envy, slander, pride, foolishness. All these evil things come from within, and they defile a man."

This book is nothing like a complete look at the sayings of the historical Jesus. It is a look at some broad themes in his teachings that carry a resonance with important lines of Christian theology. I am reviewing texts that are by format and definition new. This is usually because they are controversial. They are a part of his polemic. I am interested in texts that both are embedded in Jesus' contemporary polemic and anticipate ideas in Christianity. As a christologically orthodox Christian, I am more responsive to themes of discontinuity than to themes of continuity. Otherwise, if continuity were the main fact of his ministry, why be a Christian? Or, rather, why be a *christological* Christian?

I think of Rod Serling (1924-1975), the American writer for television. Serling grew up in a not very observant Reform Jewish family in Binghamton, New York. When he married his wife, a Protestant from an observing family, he and she "compromised" on religion, for in fact they were both religious in a broad sense. They became members of the Unitarian-Universalist Church.

Compromise in religion can be a good thing. It can prevent wars and rape. But it can also erase distinctions that are important. The "Jewish Jesus" of recent Christian interpretation is an insult to Judaism's historic protest. It is also the *coup de grâce* to orthodox Christianity. In the first instance, it makes the Jewish protest of two thousand years a tempest in a teapot. If he was fundamentally or primarily in continuity with Second Temple thought, then why did a parting of the ways take place between the two religions? Was it all an accident, created by the fall of Jerusalem and the particular openness of late Hellenistic Gentile people to ethical monotheism minus circumcision and the food laws? In the second case, the case of Christian believing, a predominantly contextualized or continuous Jesus makes Christianity into a mistake of its own. It makes Christianity into an arbitrary assertion concerning one man, the burden of which rests mainly on St. Paul. Christianity's supposed discontinuity, and most vulnerably its theological discontinuity, becomes, it has to be said, a fiction, a made-up thing.

The commitment behind this book is a commitment to discern the reason for Christianity. If there is no reason for the rise of the religion beyond reflection *ex post facto* (i.e., from Paul and the first disciples after Easter), then the religion is in trouble. Albert Schweitzer lost his faith over this point. He came to the conclusion that Jesus "as he really was" was unknowable. And what *was* knowable about Jesus was unassimilable to the modern mind. Jesus for Schweitzer became elusive. He vanished into the air. And so, for Schweitzer, did Christian believing.

But there is a further impression that drives this look at five texts, or sets of texts. It is my impression that the Reformation has been cut out of the discussion. Because Luther and the Reformers emphasized a distinction between the gospel and the Law in Christian theology, they were discontinuity people. Yes, Luther saw New Testament ideas in the Old Testament, and some Old Testament ideas in the New Testament. But Luther also saw a great divide, the greatest divide in the history of ideas, between the Law of Moses and the grace of Jesus Christ.[3] This was as fundamental a distinction for him as the distinction between the era up to John the Baptist and the era of the kingdom of heaven was for Jesus himself. Luther, together with most of the Protestant Reformers, was an antithetical thinker on this point. It was the gospel ver-

3. For a full discussion, see Heinrich Bornkamm's *Luther and the Old Testament* (Philadelphia: Fortress Press, 1969).

sus the Law. The Reformers underscored the discontinuity of Christianity.

For this reason, and also for the glaring reason that Luther wrote two anti-Jewish tracts toward the end of his life, the Reformation tradition of New Testament interpretation is out of favor today, at least among most Christian interpreters. Emphasizing the discontinuity of Christianity and especially of Jesus of Nazareth with the Second Temple period is unfashionable. It may even be wrong. It may be, too, that it is vicious.

When you downplay the antithetical structure of these texts, an antithetical structure they share with Reformation theology, you miss something. You have to explain away their antithetical substance. You have to minimize the antithetical in the heart of the text.

The five texts or groups of texts on view here are antithetical. They are unmistakably antithetical. They are set out that way, configured that way. Their plain meaning is written in the setting of an argument. What is more, they have positive links with two of the most important ideas of the Reformation, ideas that are also never fashionable and seldom widely accepted. These two ideas are original sin and *simul iustus et peccator*. They are not only basic to Protestant Reformation thought; they are basic to Christianity.

The teaching of Christ concerning purity control[4] is detailed and devastating. It is also creative. It represents human nature in a way that anticipates what in Christian theology is described as an Augustinian, Lutheran, or Jansenist view. Jesus' understanding of the person in his teaching on purity control is interior and inward, so it is parallel with the antitheses of the Sermon on the Mount. But it goes a step further, because it actually conceptualizes the human being. It describes in theoretical terms the dynamic of moral conflict, that is, of sin in relation

4. The phrase "purity control" is taken from the last episode of the first season of *The X-Files*, a once popular television show. The episode was entitled "The Erlenmayer Flask." It concerned a secret U.S. government project to create a genetically "pure" human embryo from an alien fetus. Millions of people all over the world watched the show, and millions loved it. The phrase "purity control" is apt in itself to describe what Jesus criticized in Mark, chapter 7 and Matthew, chapter 15.

to the commandments of God. Jesus' concept of persons also corrects the chronic human experience of projecting the dark side of our human nature onto something outside us rather than locating the dark side in its true space: the "heart" of man and woman. In Mark 7 and Matthew 15, the historical Jesus both conceptualizes the problem of being human and explodes the myth of projection.

How does he do this?

The teaching comes in Christ's "after class" interpretation to his students of the answer he had given to a pointed question asked him in verse 5 by the Pharisees and the scribes: "Why do your disciples not live according to the tradition of the elders, but eat with hands defiled?"

The presenting problem was that some of the disciples were not washing their hands before meals, thus breaking rules prescribed by the Law of Moses for personal hygiene. In verses 3 and 4, Mark explains for Gentile readers of his book the background to the Pharisees' and scribes' objection. Christ's answer, in verses 6, 7, and 8, which includes a quotation from Isaiah, is an *ad hominem* reply. It contrasts lip service (bad) with heart service (good). It compares the hollowness of what is said from the lips with the deeper dimension of the attitude of one's heart. The idea here is undeveloped, but still clear more or less: washing one's hands before eating should be the outward expression of an inward religious attitude. By focusing on the outward expression rather than on the inward attitude, the Pharisees and scribes have revealed that "their heart is far from me" (Isaiah 29:13).

The serious principle that drives Christ's words does not become explicit until afterwards, when he explains himself to his inner circle. Here is the breakthrough: "There is nothing outside a man which by going into him can defile him; but the things which come out of a man are what defile him" (v. 15). The idea at this point in its development is somewhat similar to Stoicism. In myself, inside myself, I am untouchable. Even if everything outside me is against me and defeating me, I — my soul, my inner thought haven — exist independent of those things. A departure from the Stoic reflex is implicit in the second half of verse 15, where Christ refers to the dimension of inwardness that "defiles." It is not just that "I" am invincible in relation to outward circumstances.

That was Marcus Aurelius's self-definition, stated again and again in the *Meditations*. But the inward "I" contains things that pollute and taint. Stoic thought does not score the insisted and invincible "fortress around my heart" with criticism, as Christ does. In Stoic thought, the actual or outward is bad and the inward is good, almost by definition. This is the "perennial philosophy" of Asian thought, as well as parts of classical Epicureanism, some Platonism and neo-Platonism, and most of Stoicism. It is all in the context here of a view held by the Pharisees and scribes that external cleanliness is the thing. For Jesus the inward is not good. It is an abscess.

Now most of the Pharisees, if pressed on this point, would have acknowledged the truth of Jesus' criticism of their question if by that criticism he was simply asking them not to focus on outward infractions of the Law but rather to see the infraction as the expression of a deeper problem of attitude. It was, after all, the heart of a person that God was after. Jesus would not have had a fight with them here in principle. But he went on to a further point when he was alone in the house with the twelve (v. 17). With this point, he parted company with the anthropology of the Pharisees and of most Second Temple thinking. He entered into a pessimistic view of human nature.

Judaism of Christ's time was not ideologically optimistic about human nature, but it was also not ideologically pessimistic about human nature. Jewish thought in the time of Christ was not a religion of Law as over against grace. It gave broad place and allowance for repentance, returning, forgiveness, restoration, and all the reparative functions of religion that Christians usually associate with their own religion.[5] In Christian terms, Judaism in almost all its schools of thought at the time of Christ was semi-Pelagian.[6] This means it saw God as basically

---

5. This whole argument concerning Jewish thought in the time of Christ was made by E. P. Sanders in *Paul and Palestinian Judaism: A Comparison of Patterns of Religion* (Philadelphia: Fortress Press, 1977).

6. The famous exception is IV Ezra. E. P. Sanders believed that IV Ezra's sin anthropology distinguishes it from all other Jewish literature of the time of Paul and Jesus. Thus Sanders writes, "In IV Ezra . . . the human inability to avoid sin is considered to lean to damnation. It is this pessimistic view of the human plight which

graceful and forgiving. But the individual still had to do his or her part. The net of second chances was wide, but you had to evince a desire to "turn from your wickedness and live" (Ezekiel 33:11).

In the historical theology of Christianity, Pelagianism[7] is the heresy that in order to be saved or accepted by God, you have to present works of ethical goodness that are acceptable to him. You have to act worthy in order to be treated as worthy. This is sometimes called "works-righteousness," a divinely approved moral character based on your (successful) efforts at being good. *Semi*-Pelagianism[8] is the teaching, also judged heretical by the church in principle[9] but extremely widespread in all times and places of the Christian movement, that your salvation or good standing before God does not depend on your works but does depend a little on them. "I get by with a little help from my friends" *(Sgt. Pepper's Lonely Hearts Club Band)*. God forgives me and wants to forgive me my sin, but he expects me to do my share. "God helps those who help themselves." He "responds" to a solid try on my part. I cannot do it all, not by a long shot. But I can show my heart is in the right place and put forth as much effort as I am capable of. And I *am* capable of some. This is semi-Pelagianism.

Much of Second Temple theology, with the exception especially of 4 Ezra, was, in Christian theological terms, semi-Pelagian. It is this

---

distinguishes the author from the rest of Judaism as it is revealed in the surviving literature" *(Paul and Palestinian Judaism,* p. 418).

7. Pelagius (c. 360-420) was a British monk who, together with Julian of Eclanum (c. 386-454), taught that the human race is able to take the first and fundamental steps towards their salvation. Pelagianism is the opposite of the teachings of Augustine of Hippo (354-430) who, together with Luther and many others, taught that the human will is inescapably bound until it is delivered from outside itself by the grace and cross of Christ.

8. Semi-Pelagianism is associated historically with theologians such as John Cassian (c. 360-after 430) and Vincent of Lerins (before 452). But it is a movement always in operation because it embodies a wish to *do something* to control one's existence.

9. Both Pelagianism and semi-Pelagianism were condemned as heretical by the ecumenical Council of Orange in 529.

semi-Pelagianism that Jesus threatens in verses 20-23 of Mark 7 and in Matthew 15:19.

An over-the-top idea, the extreme end and the point of the pen in Jesus' teachings concerning purity control, comes out here: "What comes out of a man is what defiles a man. For from within, and of the heart of man, come evil thoughts, fornication, theft, murder, adultery, coveting, wickedness, deceit, licentiousness, envy, slander, pride, foolishness. All these evil things come from within, and they defile a man" (Mark 7:20-23).

The tilt is to the dark side. The list itself of sins and sinful attitudes is long, and the repetition of the verb "defile" is striking. On the lines of this attacking concept of human personality, everyone is defiled. From this view, Paul's anthropology in Romans 3 is a short step away. The irritating Christian doctrine of original sin is present in this passage.

If there is a truly classic statement concerning original sin in the formulas of the Protestant Reformation, it is probably Article IX of the Thirty-Nine Articles of the Church of England (1563), entitled "Of Original or Birth-Sin." The writer, probably Matthew Parker, who later became Queen Elizabeth's first Archbishop of Canterbury, speaks in continuity with Jesus and in discontinuity with the semi-Pelagianism of all contexts and cultures:

> Original Sin . . . is the fault and corruption of the Nature of every man, . . . whereby man is very far gone from original righteousness, and is of his own nature inclined to evil, so that the flesh lusteth always contrary to the Spirit; and therefore in every person born into this world, it deserveth God's wrath and damnation. And this infection of nature doth remain, yea in them that are regenerated.

This *tour de force* of theological writing contains two ideas that are wholly in continuity with Christ's discontinuous concept of the human being. First, sins come from "Birth-Sin," which exists inside the man and woman and is intrinsic to human nature. The inward is a well of conflict "so that the flesh lusteth always contrary to the Spirit."

This is a pessimistic view of human character. It is in the context of a divine and gracious engagement with original sin, but it is a pessimistic view of the human situation. Article IX is wholly consistent with Mark 7 and Matthew 15.

Moreover, the fact that Christ is talking to Jews who are by definition the house of Israel, the elect of God, means that he believes that the children of God are also *at the same time* sinners and therefore children of wrath. The assumption is that you can be a child of his *and* be a person overcome by compulsions that originate inside you. That is what Luther and the Reformers meant by the phrase *simul iustus et peccator.* The Christian is saved *and* human (i.e., sinful and conflicted) simultaneously. Jesus' outlook on his hearers, those precious listeners for whom sin is still the flesh of their flesh, is Luther's exactly.

There is a further implication to the word of Christ about outward influences: "There is nothing outside a man which by going into him can defile him. . . . Do you not see that whatever goes into a man from outside cannot defile him, since it enters not his heart but his stomach, and so passes on?" (Mark 7:15, 18-19).

Jesus does not therefore pronounce all foods clean, as Mark wants to add in verse 19b, although that is a possible inference. What Jesus does do is pull the rug out from under the compulsion to project. You cannot have a corrected view of human problems, you cannot discern the origin of evil within the heart and spirit of the man and woman, and then turn around and blame somebody else. To do that would be unsatisfactory and untrue. A non-projecting philosophy of human sin makes you responsible before God, and allergic, in theory, to scapegoating. No one likes to hear this, at least not initially.

It was reported that the George Gallup organization once took a poll of Americans and found that 300 percent of them consider themselves to be victims! Christ's teaching here parts company, so disturbingly and uncomfortably, with the experience of blaming as to make it possible to imagine how a violent resistance to his ministry could have developed. Jesus' failure to honor the "normal" inclination to project blame outside the person onto a vexing and oppressing circumstance is a primary cause of the resistance to him then and to Christian anthropology now.

We could say that the strenuous and unflattering interpretation of human character that is all wrapped up in this creates the climate for atonement, the need for a savior. As a Christian, I cannot resist the deduction. But in the historical Jesus' teaching itself, the plain thing, the unmistakable kernel, is that original sin is humanity's definition, that the sin inheres to our flesh and blood even when our relation to God is sound, and that projecting sin onto someone or something else is a form of self-deception.

The teaching of the historical Jesus concerning purity control is a bold performance, a heuristic point in time, a Christian U-turn in the history of ideas. It is a development that takes conventional teaching, Gentile and Jewish, two, maybe three full steps into a new universe. This is the First Christian creating.

Calling Sinners: Matthew 9:10-13; Mark 2:15-17; Luke 5:29-32; also Luke 5:33-34 (and Parallels)

And as he sat at table in the house, behold, many tax collectors and sinners came and sat down with Jesus and his disciples. And when the Pharisees saw this, they said to his disciples, "Why does your teacher eat with tax collectors and sinners?" And when he heard it, he said, "Those who are well have no need of a physician, but those who are sick. . . . For I came not to call the righteous but sinners." (Matthew 9:10-13)

And as he sat at table in his house, many tax collectors and sinners were sitting with Jesus and his disciples; for there were many who followed him. And the scribes of the Pharisees, when they saw that he was eating with sinners and tax collectors, said to his disciples, "Why does he eat with tax collectors and sinners?" And when Jesus heard it, he said to them, "Those who are well have no need of a physician, but those who are sick. I came not to call the righteous, but sinners." (Mark 2:15-17)

And Levi made him a great feast in his house; and there was a large company of tax collectors and others sitting at table with them. And the Pharisees and their scribes murmured against his disciples, saying, "Why do you eat and drink with tax collectors and sinners?" And Jesus answered them, "Those who are well have no need of a physician, but those who are sick; I have not come to call the righteous, but sinners to repentance." (Luke 5:29-32)

And they said to him, "The disciples of John fast often and offer prayers, and so do the disciples of the Pharisees, but yours eat and drink." And Jesus said to them, "Can you make wedding-guests fast while the bridegroom is with them?" (Luke 5:33-34; cf. Mark 2:18-19 and Matthew 9:14-15)

The three forms found in Matthew, Mark, and Luke of Jesus' call to sinners rather than to the righteous are almost identical. Only in Luke is there a specific *Sitz im Leben,* or setting. The setting in Luke is the feast of the tax collector Levi. My point is that Christ's assertion, which is not a parable or a question but a plain descriptive statement, is so rooted in the basic story that it resists any editing or changes. The Christianness of Matthew 9, Mark 2, and Luke 5 is fixed in the maxim, "I came not to call the righteous, but sinners to repentance." It is an either-or statement consisting of a negation and an affirmation. The negation consists in what Christ does not do; the affirmation consists in what he does. He does not come to address the righteous. To those people, he has nothing to say. He is not an instructor to those inside the house of faith. He is a piper to those outside the house. He pipes to the sinners.

The implications of Christ's statement are Christian ones. He has nothing to offer the observants, the adepts, the mystics, those in training, and those in pursuit of the good. It is not that he hates them or even dismisses them. But his field of vision is on the failures and the stumblers. This is similar to the parable of the prodigal son, in which his focus is on the son who acts out and limps home a disaster, rather than on the son who stays at home, flies right, and is always with the father and his love (Luke 15). Despite three decades now of Sunday sermons in which the elder brother's fate in the parable is emphasized, the plain word of the parable, its focus, is on the prodigal. It is not on the elder brother. The words to the elder brother are an important afterthought, but they are not the focus. The focus is on the offending son.

Similarly, Jesus says nothing disparaging about the "righteous" in his statement of his call. But he does say that they, the righteous, are not his object in coming. The sinners are his object. Here we are in the "narrow ground," which is really a broad and high ground, of God's justification of the godless, which was Ernst Käsemann's shorthand for the Protestant Reformers' "justification by faith." He came to call sinners to repentance. This is the *iustificatio impiorum*.

The discontinuity here is with a divine program that works *with* the believer. The discontinuity is with every form of semi-Pelagianism that has ever existed.

The continuity, on the other hand, is with non-believers or, better, non-achievers. The continuity is with what we today call "Type-B's," and also perhaps "Type-A's in recovery"! The continuity is with the religion of 1 Corinthians 1:27-29: "for God chose what is foolish in the world to shame the wise, . . . God chose what is low and despised in the world, even things that are not, to bring to nothing things that are, so that no human being might boast in the presence of God."

The once well-known phrase "option for the poor," from the theology of liberation of the 1960s and '70s, is right here, in Matthew 9:13, Mark 2:17, and Luke 5:32. Luther's 1536 *Disputation on Man*, which dismantles human pride to reconstruct it on a new foundation (i.e., *iustificatio impiorum ex fide*), is right here. The whole historic Christian interest in the poor, the alcoholic, the prisoner, the converted thief, the madonna of the streetwalkers, the African slave, and the "untouchable" caste: it is all right here. Nor is it implicit or centrifugal or anonymous. It is right here, fully fleshed.

But there is something more to say. Each of the Gospels sets this especially Christian axiom of Christ in the eschatological context of the controversy with John the Baptist. The setting of the saying, which is as anchored in memory as the saying itself, is crucial for understanding the origin of Christianity, which is the issue of this book.

Christ called the sinners to the feast, that is, to the kingdom of heaven, because now was the time. Not later, when the final judgment had come; nor sooner, when the old promissory dispensation of John and his forerunners was in effect. But now, "when the bridegroom is with them" (Luke 5:34; Matthew 9:15; and Mark 2:19).

Here is the edge, the extreme end, of Jesus' contribution. All cats are gray in the twilight, which is the "meantime" of Christ's presence between John and the (second) coming of the Son of Man. Christ sees sinners under the same divine lamp as the righteous. Thus you love your enemies because (a) you do not know exactly who they are, or which exactly of the world's people are bad and which are good; and (b) God makes the final decision, not you, so in anticipation you treat them all alike. You stay in your place and avoid a mistake. You treat everyone the same, just as the rain and sun do (Matthew 5:45).

Yet even in the antitheses of the Sermon on the Mount, one observes movement: movement from the love of all to the particular love of the enemies. It is as if the counterintuitive love of the enemy were the only way to love everyone alike. For the enemy is the most discordant category. If you love your enemy, you will love everybody, because you already love your friends.

Now, here, in the "time when the bridegroom is with them," this is the time for the feast of *sinners*. The righteous are not at the feast. The focus for Jesus of Nazareth is on the sinners. Christ's focus narrows here, you could almost say. It is not on everybody but on those who could be classified as the worst. This is the key to William Booth, who founded the Salvation Army. The blind, the halt, and the lame go in first, before "you." "I tell you, many will come from east and west and sit at table with Abraham, Isaac, and Jacob in the kingdom of heaven, while the sons of the kingdom will be thrown into the outer darkness; there men will weep and gnash their teeth" (Matthew 8:11-12).

The seed of Christianity's concentration on the "off-scouring of the world" (1 Corinthians 4:13) is found here, and not only its seed, but the soil in which it grew. Jesus' Christianity came directly out of his separation from John. But the seeds carried within them the chain-reaction of a fission that is still taking place, bursting norms and projections about people in every generation, and sometimes again breaking through, as in the abolition movement of the eighteenth and nineteenth centuries, in fields that were previously quiet and fallow.

The five texts or themes that have been represented in this chapter are *de facto* creative and discontinuous. The kingdom of heaven's being at hand in the first call to repentance declares a change. The exorcisms declare a mighty advent and a change. The antitheses of Matthew 5 depict a new view of the Law. Christ's approach to "purity control" is stated in controversy and attacks the superficiality of concentrating on the deed at the expense of the source. The inflammatory word, not just *for* the "bad" but also *against* the "good," is uncomfortable and dissonant.

Moreover, all five themes and assertions are a function of between-times. When the Son of Man comes in his glory, when the bridegroom actually arrives to meet the bride, then the deeds and signs of the time between will end. At that time, when the third and last word of the plan is revealed, all bets will be off. No more love of enemy required, no more call to the sinners only. This is because the dragnet's catch will be culled, the net cleaned, and the bad fish thrown into the sea. Then on the last day, in its true appearance, it will be over.

Until then, however, it is a time of repentance, of purging foul demons, of inward analysis and self-criticism, of humility before the noisome "heart" of man and woman, and of focus on sinners.

The implications for Christian theology of these five original themes come next. The rich implications of Christ's insights, born from the impasse with John, for the future thought of the world are easy to see. Once you see the between-times ideas of Christ in their fantastic newness, the origins of the Christian way of life and its anthropology in the light of Christology are not hard to place. The centrifugal force of Christ's statements made Christianity what it became.

• 5 •

The Centrifugal Force of Jesus the Christian

Historicist Theology

In order to keep faith with its roots, systematic theology has to be historicist. Its statements have got to be rooted in history. If the statements of systematic theology are not rooted in history, in the things that really happened, then they are constructions. Do we need more constructions in the world, a world in which every human being is constructing reality as he or she goes along? Subjectivity rules in shaping personal truth. What is able to make one viewer's truth more perceptive than the next? We should distrust theology that is not historicist, for its creativity is unverifiable in every instance.

This book calls historicism good. Historicism is the urge to anchor theological ideas in events that once took place. Historicist theology connects unconditional universal truths to conditional facts. Big ideas grow hollow unless they grow from tangible seeds. The seeds of Christian theology are in the life of the historical Jesus.

To be sure, the historical Jesus is not the limit of theology. But he is the core of it. He is the grounds for it. As Käsemann said, "He is the Evangelist without qualification." Christianity as Christians know it comes from Christ. I cannot wish to present and know a version of it that is not tied historically to him. To put it another way, Christians will recognize in the one who lived then, the one whom they love and adore now.

Lessing's famous critique of historicism, that facts are too flimsy a foundation for faith, has an adolescent ring to it. It sounds like someone who has just discovered for the first time the distinction between universals and particulars. Yes, Christ was a particular man, and yes, Christianity is a universal worldview. But the abstract is deduced from the concrete. The specific or concrete in this case, the historical Jesus, birthed the new age of Christianity's transnational movement. To separate the two things, the individual founder from the decontextualizing mass movement, is not true to life.

The Gospel writers would never have written their biographies of the man had they for a single second recognized such a separation. No conscious Christian would become such if he were not convinced that his trust were on solid ground. The old common-room tradition in English apologetics — Who moved the stone?; Evidence for the Resurrection; "Jesus: Liar, Lunatic, or Lord?" — has something to teach us still. Did these things happen or did they not? Did he rise? Did he love? Did he heal? If such things did not take place, then why be or become a Christian? If they did take place, then this is definitely "evidence that demands a verdict" (Josh McDowell).

It is just so plain and obvious that principles rest on facts. Lessing's "discovery" sounds mischievous and pretentious. It is also condescending to the universe of people who understand the facts, in their relation to theology, in a more positive way.

Granted there is no one-to-one correlation between facts and faith. But there is no clean break in the connection, either. The more you study the Gordian knot statements of Christ, the polemical ones especially, you can see the roots and veins of Augustinian, Lutheran, and Jansenist theology, the trunk-lines of Christology and anthropology so radically and creatively uncovered at the Reformation.

Was the Protestant summons *ad fontes* a mistake? Was it misconceived? No! It was the compulsion laid on all seekers for truth to find out if the things asserted are in fact the case. There is nothing intrinsically atheistic in the Gershwin song from *Porgy and Bess,* "It Ain't Necessarily So."

That song cuts both ways. It ain't necessarily so, about Jonah and the whale. But it ain't necessarily *not* so, until it is demonstrated.

Returning to first principles always gets down to the strengths and weaknesses of a thing. Anything short of this is in danger of being a construction. The medieval church and its schoolmen were involved in a fantastic construction. Underneath, there was something important and invaluably worthy. But everything on top had to be scrapped in order to get down to what lay beneath the surface. The Reformers' view of the Bible was historicist. Their impulse was *ad origines*. That is the impulse of this book, historicist and critical.

A Time for Universals

Before setting out the main themes of the centrifugal theology of Jesus the First Christian, there is something else that needs to be said concerning particularity in relation to universality within our world of the early twenty-first century. It is related to a foundation concept of this book, the relation of discontinuity to continuity.

Much attention today is focused on particularity. The journalistic term for this is "balkanization." Everything is divided and subdivided into individualizing definitions. I am a "middle-class conservative college student of non-Hispanic origin" or a "disabled male triathlete" or a "Caucasian woman married with children." Specific labels that have to do with identity are considered meaningful and important. We think of this as "political correctness." But there is more to it than that. Universals, or universal descriptions for things, are distrusted. They swallow up, put down, and reduce to insignificance particular experiences of particular human beings. It is common "neo-conservative" sentiment to regard canons and standards and quality and accepted ideas of the good as having become swamped and buried by postmodern particularizing political correctness. Absolutes are trumped by perspectivalism.

The reason for particularity's dominance is a normal human rebellion against the suppressions wrought by generations of generalizing idea-makers. It was the generalizers, after all, the "dead white males," who neglected the achievements of women for centuries and centuries. It was the generalizers who never talked about the "Harlem Renaissance," or the "B" and "C" movies of the 1950s that reflected vibrant culture just as accurately as the "A" movies. It is the generalizers who let lie in complete obscurity Joe Meek, the first independent record-producer who ever worked in England. Meek changed the world of recorded sound! It is the generalizers who almost missed and almost made everyone else miss the Gothic tales of South American women and the voices of Polish poetry during the Cold War.

No wonder we are skeptical concerning generalizers, the guardians of universal concepts of truth and beauty. The debate over the general and universal versus the concrete and particular is important. The future of divided countries like South Africa and Northern Ireland, or for that matter California in the U.S.A., is related to this question.

A current controversy in Northern Ireland embodies the issue. The prevailing cultural policy from the British government in Ulster in recent years has been to speak of the "two communities": the Protestants, the bare majority, of 53 percent; and the Catholics, the minority, of 44 percent. Each community is affirmed, at least in principle, although the Catholics get the lion's share of affirmation at present, partly as "reparation" for the past. Each community receives funding and community workers and grants for education, etc.[1] *Cross*-community work, then, becomes the commended good, the acme of aspiration. Cross-

---

1. An example of this is the Fernhill Museum in Belfast. Seldom visited by tourists and almost unknown even in Northern Ireland, this fascinating museum is a showcase of Protestant/Loyalist/Unionist/Orange culture. It was founded to give one community a vehicle for self-expression. It is an advocacy museum, not an "objective" display case for artifacts.

Evangelical religious tracts lie in stacks by the ticket desk, local partisan newspapers are sold, and the exhibits attempt to tell a story that is rarely told, at least to the general public and through the media. The "docents," which is an American term that does not apply to this museum, have tattoos on their arms and rings in their ears. The experience of the Fernhill Museum is authentic, particular, not "objective," and strikingly alien to generalizers. The Fernhill Museum — may it prosper — is the plus side of particularity.

community projects are projects that bring together representatives from both the Protestant and Catholic communities for a common end.

Even so, the idea of the two communities is under fire. The criticism leveled against the idea is that it stresses duality over unity, and in so doing perpetuates it. Far better, say the critics of the two-community model, to speak of *one* country, *one* people, *one* harmony.

The jury is out on the theory of two communities in Northern Ireland, but the situation is a textbook example of the particular versus the general in their continuing tension.

Christianity is a religion that weighs in on the side of the general. This is demonstrated in a classic text from the epistles of St. Paul, Galatians 3:28: "There is neither Jew nor Greek, there is neither slave nor free, there is neither male nor female; for you are all one in Christ Jesus." From the earliest days, Christianity stressed the superiority of a single specific, Christ Jesus, over all other concepts of human identity. The particularities of race and ethnicity (i.e., Jew and Gentile), power (i.e., slave and free), and gender (i.e., male and female) vanish under the tidal wave of one universal person.

The whole movement of Christianity is away from the particular and toward the general. For this reason, Christianity is in tension with the particularizing trend of present-day thought.

In another era, if totalitarian governments got the upper hand in majority-Christian countries, then Christianity would be in tension with the general. In Soviet Russia and still in China today, Christianity opts for the individual and the characteristic over the state and the collective. But in hyper-particularizing, individuating cultures such as the U.S.A., Christianity shifts toward its generalizing side. It shifts toward its unitive, reconciling, barriers-lowering side. It does this in order to be true to itself.

That is why the study of Jesus today needs to reconnect with the universal part, with its distinctions-reducing theme. I do not dismiss the particularities of Christ in context. He was a Jew of the Second Temple period and spoke almost exclusively to Jews of the Second Temple period. The fact is *selbstverständlich*. But we miss an important contribution that Christianity is able to make to world culture when we evade its universalizing impulse.

We are rightly warned not to generalize from our own experience. The warning stands, *except* in the case of someone of insight, such as Freud or Luther. Those two had such profound life experiences, and were given to reflect on those experiences so profoundly, that we are able to accept many of their observations as universal. Of course we would miss something if we refused to look at their personal biographies as the seedbed for their resonant ideas. Thus Freud may have been off base on the specifics of infants' sexuality, but his dynamic discovery of the unconscious is confirmed over and over again in clinical observation and experience. Thus Luther may have judged too harshly certain aspects of Catholicism, but his penetration regarding guilt, judgment, and despair is untradeable. Millions read his own accounts of an inner life as if it were their own. "Luther was a patient of great significance for Europe" (Kierkegaard). In the case of Jesus of Nazareth, we do an injustice to ourselves when we paint out the universal appeals and summonses.

All this is why we need to be historicist in New Testament research for the precise reason of grounding, and strengthening, the universals.

Paradoxically, the universals of the "historical Jesus" are identical with his discontinuities. Jesus' discontinuities with Judaism are of vital interest to Christians, for they are the material of his continuity with Christianity as a whole, by which Christianity overrides ethnic identities and every single context capable of existing. Christ's discontinuities with his context are the substance of his continuity with the religion that carries his name. While there is a self-evident and demonstrable continuity of many of his sayings with rabbinic ideas and texts, their continuity is not on the Christian side. The discontinuity weighs in by definition on the universalizing side. Jesus' discontinuous principles are the centrifugal material of everything that came later.

The Theology of Jesus the Christian

This is the theology of the discontinuous Jesus, the First Christian, the universalizer of monotheism whose first principles arose from a single difference in emphasis with John the Baptist. This is the systematic religious worldview of the historical Jesus.

The Key Imperative in Human Existence:
The Summons to Repent (Matthew 4:17)

The only thing that a man and woman can do in the interests of their position or stake in the kingdom of God is to analyze their dividedness, self-deception, and paralysis. Repentance — which means the diagnosis of one's always being in the wrong in the face of God — is the characteristic human act. What can we *do* to contribute to our pleading, desperate hope for a place in God's kingdom? What are we in a position to offer? Only our devastated confession.

This rules out Pelagian Christianity, which is the idea that I can make myself saveable and thus attractive to God. It rules out semi-Pelagian Christianity, which is the idea that God helps me in titanic areas of my insufficiency, but in other less desolated or weakened areas I can do it by myself. Semi-Pelagianism is the old Blues number by Charles Musslewhite: "You gotta help me. I can't do it by myself."

Repentance is the defining human act, the existential definition of what it means to be a man or woman. Jesus' centering on this act expunges all theologies of effort and also of willpower. His theology is evangelical absolutely because it is an address to the "damned sinner" (Luther on Psalm 51). There is no other person to whom the invitation to repent communicates. The anthropology here is unequivocally breaking. It is non-Tridentine, hence Protestant; non-Jesuit, hence Jansenist; and non-Pelagian and non–semi-Pelagian, hence Augustinian. Moreover, because the eschatology of Christ is open-ended — we do not know the hour of the Son of Man — the blistering demand of judgment can actually be absorbed, that is, responded to in depth.

Jesus' call was to repentance, yet there was time. His theology was absolutely penitential.

Repentance in the Light of God's Final Victory (Luke 11:20)

The exorcisms are a sort of prelude to enabled repentance. Self-criticism is impossible for persons who exist in the kingdom of wrath and not of grace. We all know that painful truths cannot be faced in an atmosphere of judgment. Repentance never happens within an atmosphere of judgment. Grace, which is accurately defined as unconditional love, is part of the prelude or prerequisite of confession.

What I mean is that life and catastrophe and mourning and loss judge us. They reduce us. They reduce us to the beginnings of repentance, honest viewing into what is true about our state. But repentance has to exist in some relation to hope. Repentance divorced from any possibility of a new beginning is impossible.

The exorcisms of Christ are the "finger of God" (Exodus 31:18), verifying the Messenger's connection with Power. The Power is against evil and personal demons. It is a constructive divine Power joined to a call, "Repent!," by which our normal hopes for ourselves are deconstructed. The dismantling Law of God linked with the benign Power unleashed against the personal demons is the ground floor of Christian theological existence. Repentance without the exorcizing Power is fruitless and also impossible. If it did exist, if there were such a thing as repentance cut loose from the intention to save, it would engender suicide.

Frank Lake, the English psychiatrist and theologian, saw this principle clearly. He wrote of the Freudian "death-wish" when it is unaccompanied by the crucified Christ:

> It may be, as orthodox analytic theory implies, that God has cursed the whole human species at genetic level with an innate death instinct, a built-in drive which can always be relied on to

hate and oppose the organisms striving for life, with self-destructive intensity. . . . Yet Job's lively argument with a God who persecutes is preferable to an insidious poisoning of the wells of life itself by a constant seepage of a dark death instinct, drawing all things into its destructive embrace.[2]

Lake's "lively argument with God" refers to a conversation opened rather than a door shut. The address in the New Testament to human beings to repent is in the way of just such a two-way conversation. The exorcisms are annunciating and prevenient. They give the possibility and enacted hope of new life in the face of the most far-gone circumstances.

Sin Is Material, Not Formal; Sin Is Psycho-Genetic, Ontological, and Original; Ethics Is the Science of Motives, Not Actions (Matthew 5:21-47)

The Christology of Christianity is centrifugal within the historical Jesus, but not *as* centrifugal as its anthropology and its soteriology. The uniqueness of Christ's person is implicit in his self-presentation as the new Moses, the one who speaks antithetically in the fifth chapter of Matthew's Gospel. But there are several steps from the new Moses to the incarnate Son of God. There is an even further distance to the second person of the Trinity. But the new Moses is a short step away from the anthropology of Paul, Augustine, Luther, and Pascal. This is because of the inwardness of sin's grasp on the person as it is diagnosed in the antitheses of the Sermon on the Mount.

When interaction is disconnected from action, anthropology becomes superficial. It lacks "nuance." Second Temple applications of the Law of Moses were tolerant and not impervious to new beginnings and capitulation on the part of the sinner in consequent favor of restoration. But Jesus' heightening of the demand to include the suppressed

2. Frank Lake, "The Theology of Pastoral Counselling," *Contact* 68 (1980): 3.

unconscious — that was extreme. Add to his strengthening of the demand on the total inward the unexceptionability of the decree to stay married and not divorce, and apply to all that the further conceptual stipulation of Matthew 5:48, and we have a fully developed theology of original sin.

Christ's centrifugal theology resists almost every single word of casuistry that ever came from the Jesuit order during the Counter-Reformation period. Suarez (1548-1617) and Molina (1535-1600) were the antithesis of Jesus' antitheses. The Jansenist fathers were justified by the human self-portrait given in the antitheses of Christ. The dark diagnostic brilliance of Christianity's view of humankind is justified in relation to the Sermon on the Mount.

A whole spiritual tradition is opened up here in the words of Christ concerning psychic anger, concupiscence, the identity of every neighbor in the eyes of God, and the mandate for God-likeness, which can only produce knee-jerk appalledness in relation to the legacy of God-*un*-likeness.

Pertinent to Christianity's poor profile among secular modernists is this issue of psycho-genetic sin and its relation to guilt. When you ask most critics of Christianity what it is fundamentally to which they object, it often comes down to their idea that Christianity is guilt-inducing, negative, and judgmental. I am not sure if I have ever encountered a single case of allergy to the Christian religion that has not been some function of reaction, often stemming from puberty and adolescence, against the perception that Christianity rejects sex, pleasure, and personal fulfillment and expression.

What is being objected to, from innumerable experiences of perceived criticism and rejection coming from the direction of Christianity, which becomes the very incarnation on earth of the superego, is an understanding of sin and wrath that is not profound. The antitheses consist of a diagnosis of moral failure that is webbed to the bloodstream and bowels of the individual. The antitheses regard the human person as a system in which everything is a unity. When a red light comes on in the basement, alarms go off on every floor.

E. P. Sanders told me he "got off the boat" of Christianity when he discerned that the evangelical churches' fixation on minor sexual sins was an untruth. Those particular sins weren't that bad! But Sanders's experience of the churches, repeated characteristically in the lives of so many skeptical Christian scholars who seem homogeneously to emerge from conservative Christian milieus, is a clue to something. It is a powerful clue to the fact that *Christ's Christianity teaches no such thing.* Christ's Christianity is a whole consistent existential impression of the human situation as bound, as implicated subrationally and also rationally in overmastering drives, as paralyzed and as needing to be saved. That does not mean simply needing to be saved in one's sexual life, or in one's life in court, or in one's ambivalence toward one's parents (see the "Corban" passage of Mark 7:9-13; cf. Matthew 15:4-5), but needing to be saved in one's whole being and essence.

The Jesuit structure of guilt processing that surrounds sacramental confession, or the "reconciliation of a penitent" as it is now called, the whole theater of penance and satisfaction issuing from the seventeenth century in Spain and France — that structure is what creates the reaction to Christianity that many believe is endemic to being Christian. On the Protestant side, it is the "thou shalt nots" of evangelicalism that have promoted the reaction and hatred so common in writers and critics and artists. Christianity becomes the enemy because its moral focus is understood to be formal rather than material, attending to outward actions rather than to the infinitely more important inward motive.

I focus on the anthropology of Christianity because it is an area where faith goes wrong. The antitheses of the First Christian are in fact a Freudian position of depth that explains the world. The antitheses explain the First World War, the Holocaust, Rwanda, addictions, and the numberless lawsuits that shatter families, together with the second marriages that damage worlds and generations of people. The antitheses explain the captivity of individuals who are mastered by forces they do not understand, wrestled to the ground by irruptions of impulsive emotion that mow down the ones they love or thought they loved.

The antitheses also exhibit the anthropology of *iustus et peccator,* the individuation of original sin by which a divided person remains divided even after being saved. The division within every person, the conflict that comes out every day, is a theological fact: believers are loved (saved) and human (sinners) at the same time. George Herbert (1593-1633) observed this in his poem "Giddiness":

> Oh, what a thing is man! how farre from power
>> From settled peace and rest!
> He is some twentie sev'rall men at least
>> Each sev'rall hour.

The centrifugal force of the antitheses is the teaching of original sin, the one empirically verifiable Christian idea.

Understand, too, that this teaching, going directly back to the historical Jesus, refutes a characteristic American idea, the idea of "free will," or Arminianism as it is termed in historical theology. So often, sincere Christians, Catholic and Protestant, refer to something they call the "doctrine of free will." They have not been taught that *there is no such doctrine.* It is true that after 1711, the year when the Church of Rome officially rejected Augustinianism, Catholic teaching began to sound as if the Church taught "free will." But in fact, the idea that a person has "free will" to choose the good over the bad was almost everywhere in Christianity understood to be a heresy until 1711.[3]

Christians, like everybody else, enjoy believing that they possess "free will," the freedom to do what they want. But experience, and certainly the words of Christ in his antitheses, contest this idea down the line. All you need to do is consider the addicted, the touchy, the alcoholic, the angry, the rebellious, the conforming, and you see that the

---

3. This is clear from the Council of Orange (529) and also from every one of the official Reformation confessions of the sixteenth century. See, for example, Article X, "Of Free Will," of the Anglican Church's Thirty-Nine Articles:

> The condition of Man after the fall of Adam is such, that he cannot turn and prepare himself, by his own natural strength and good works, to faith, and calling upon God. Wherefor we have no power to do good works pleasant and acceptable to God, without the grace of God by Christ preventing us [i.e., going before us — PZ], that we may have a good will, and working with us, when we have that good will.

freedom people want to have is much more limited than they think. Empirical observation contradicts the conviction that people wish to convey to themselves that they are free. The American film masterpiece *Magnolia* (2000) is an assault on the idea that people possess "free will."

But we did not have to wait for *Magnolia!* It was all in the antitheses.

"Total Depravity" (Mark 7:10-23; Matthew 15:1-20)

"Total depravity" is not and never has been the idea it is normally represented to be. It is not the idea that the human race is totally depraved. It is, rather, the idea that not one corner of a person is outside the reach of original sin. Our depravedness reaches into every pore. There are no non-sinful outposts inside a person. Every island in the stream needs to be evangelized, for every continent is dark.

The most striking thing about Christ's pronouncements concerning "purity control" is their weight on the negative side. They offer no glimpse into the origin of St. Paul's "fruit of the Spirit" (Galatians 5:22-23). Rather, they major on the "works of the flesh" (Galatians 5:19-21): evil thoughts, fornication, theft, murder, adultery, coveting, wickedness, deceit, licentiousness, envy, slander, pride, foolishness (Mark 7:21-22; Matthew 15:19).

While the antitheses uncover the inner uncontrollables, the words about "purity control" define them and describe them in their dark colors. Christ's tendency is to the most extreme point of diagnosis. Under the rock are rattlers, not chameleons; scorpions, not slugs.

The anthropology of Christ is not just "nuanced," a glimpse into ambiguity and the dynamic theory of human personality. It is stronger than that. It defines the nuance of character in the terms of an Edgar Allan Poe. The well is not just deep. It is the well at the bottom of the abbot's garden in M. R. James's chilling short story entitled "The Treasure of Abbot Thomas." When the antiquarian in the story lowers himself into the well to remove the gold he believes is buried there, he thinks he has found it. But he also finds, in the pitch-dark narrowed space, a furry, slimy, supernatural creature who kisses him in the most horrifying embrace. He is lucky to get out alive. Will he ever be able to sleep again?[4]

Similarly, the abscess of human depth — which Jesus conjures up privately to his students "in the house," after he has said publicly that ritual washing is irrelevant because the dirt to be expunged is inexpungeable — is infected. The abscess is not neutral. I say this to underscore, as the text underscores, the pessimistic view of human nature that Jesus held.

Jesus' view of human nature carries with it two possible responses: suicide or salvation.

The Soteriology of the "Historical Jesus"
(Matthew 9:10-15; Mark 2:15-19; Luke 5:29-35)

Just as Christ's anthropology was weighted toward the negative, so his ministry was tilted toward the sinners. Christ said that he did not come to call the righteous. This is a strong operating definition that functions by means of a negation. It is not a deduction, nor is it an inference. Christ did not come to call those who did not need him. By the same logic that only sick people line up to see the doctor, so only the lapsed and the lawbreakers came to him. Someone else would deal with the good people. His call was to the bad ones.

---

4. See M. R. James's *'Casting the Runes' and Other Ghost Stories* (Oxford and New York: Oxford University Press, 1987), pp. 78-96.

The climax of the tale, in which an expected "treasure" turns to malevolence, is worth quoting:

> Well, I felt to the right, and my fingers touched something curved, that felt — yes — more or less like leather; dampish it was, and evidently part of a heavy, full thing. There was nothing, I must say, to alarm one. I grew bolder and putting both hands in as well as I could I pulled it to me, and it came. It was heavy, but moved more easily than I had expected. . . . I went on pulling out the great bag in complete darkness. It hung for an instant on the edge of the hole, then slipped forward on to my chest and *put its arms round my neck.* (p. 94, emphasis original)

Soteriology is the way and means of saving a person. "What must I do to be saved?" (Acts 16:30). It is the way and means of rescuing a person from deadly threat. It presupposes that the threat menacing you is so serious that it requires outside intervention to get you free of it and prevent your dying because of it.

Christ's soteriology is focused and exclusive. It is focused on sinners and prodigal sons, not on elder brothers. It is exclusive to sinners. This is because "those who are well have no need of a physician" (Matthew 9:12; Mark 2:17; Luke 5:31). The non-inclusive and non-universal voice is not a slap at other religions, such as Buddhism and Islam. The non-inclusive factor is instead a barrier to the non-needy people, or better, to the needy people who do not realize they are needy. The radical soteriology in play is based on the anthropology: trouble in paradise to the core and root of human nature.

Of all Christ's ideas, his soteriology has had the most powerful centrifugal force. It drew immediately to itself the dregs of the world. "For consider your call, brothers; not many of you were wise according to worldly standards, not many were powerful, not many were of noble birth; but God chose what is foolish in the world to shame the wise, God chose what is weak in the world to shame the strong, God chose what is low and despised in the world, even things that are not, to bring to nothing things that are" (1 Corinthians 1:26-28).

E. R. Dodds, the British classicist, concerned himself with an important question all through his study of early Christianity entitled *Pagan and Christian in an Age of Anxiety*.[5] Dodds's question was this: What accounts for the rapid spread of Christianity, its triumphant spread through the world of late Hellenistic antiquity, the vast world of the Roman empire? What was the appeal of Christianity? Dodds came up with this answer. His book is justifiably famous:

Epictetus has described for us the dreadful loneliness that can beset a man in the midst of his fellows (Epictetus 3:13.1-3). Such

5. E. R. Dodds, *Pagan and Christian in an Age of Anxiety* (Cambridge: Cambridge University Press, 1965).

loneliness must have been felt by millions — the urbanised tribesman, the peasant come to town in search of work, the demobilised soldier, the rentier ruined by inflation, and the manumitted slave. For people in that situation membership of a Christian community might be the only way of maintaining their self-respect and giving their life some semblance of meaning. Within the community there was human warmth: someone was interested in them, both here and hereafter. It is therefore not surprising that the earliest and the most striking advances of Christianity were made in the great cities — in Antioch, in Rome, in Alexandria. Christians were in a more than formal sense "members one of another": I think that was a major cause, perhaps the strongest single cause, of the spread of Christianity.[6]

It was the love and community encountered by loose-ended people in the home churches of earliest Christianity that E. R. Dodds believed to be the appeal. The people whom St. Paul addresses in 1 Corinthians 1 were the focus of the religion, the many who were not "wise," not "noble," not "influential." This is the negation within Christ's exclusive soteriology. The wise, the noble, and the influential, the "righteous," were not the people toward whom Christ directed his work. Christ came for the sinners. This is the authentic view of the Christian soteriology: toward sinners, not the righteous.

Look at this theme in Christian history and self-understanding. It was the organizing principle in the spread of Christianity. Soteriology was the magnet. It is the attractor in vertical terms, reassuring all wounded cast-off spirits that God will take them up. It has been the attractor in horizontal terms, that a group of compassionate friends will take them up. The attraction of the soteriology is captured in novels about earliest Christianity such as *Quo Vadis* and *Ben Hur,* even *The Robe.* It is captured in the movie versions of those classics, even in Hollywood's *Quo Vadis,* the least of them. It is captured surprisingly and brilliantly in Fritz Lang's 1926 *Metropolis,* in which the hero is guided down

6. Dodds, *Pagan and Christian,* pp. 137-38.

into the tunnels and burrows of the subterranean city where the oppressed anonymous workers live. There, at the deepest layer of the nether world where the city's legions of tired laborers exist, the hero is ushered into a Christian liturgy, where a cross and a speaker voice hope. His true love is also there!

Lang's imagery is taken from the catacombs, beneath the city of Rome, where the Christians in antiquity buried their dead. Remember that reverent burial was a basic need never covered for the lowest of the low in Roman society. Either you were the dues-paying member of a craft guild, like AFTRA or the teachers' union, which took care of your body and your family at the end, or you were not. Unless you were wealthy or professional, your last remains were of interest to no one. Christianity took loving care of this most basic need among the underclass. The house-church or community was the horizontal form of Christ's vertical soteriology to "the sinners."[7]

The centrifugal force of Jesus' soteriology is discerned in the cyclical movements of renewal that have rejuvenated Christianity since the earliest days. Christianity was renewed by the Montanists, by the Franciscans, by the Lollards, by the Hussites; by the Protestant Reformers, who gave everything to reemphasize Christ's soteriology; by John Wesley and the Methodists; by William Booth and the Salvation Army; by the ecumenical charismatic movement of the late twentieth century. All these involved a rediscovery of soteriology, the saving dimension in personal terms.

He did not call the righteous. I do not understand "church-renewal" movements, such as the Counter-Reformation and the Oxford Movement, to be included on the list of soteriological re-starts that have enabled Christianity to burst out again and again in fresh contexts. Movements of praise, movements of reverence, movements of

---

7. See Roger Gehring's authoritative study of early Christian house-churches: *Hausgemeinde und Mission. Die Bedeutung antiker Häuser und Hausgemeinschaften von Jesus bis Paulus* (Brunnen: TVG, 2000).

For a poignant and stirring recreation in literature of an early Christian house-church, see Chapter 23 ("Divine Service") of Walter Pater's 1885 novel *Marius the Epicurean* (London/New York: Everyman's Library, 1966), pp. 214-20.

sublime beauty, movements of retrenching, movements of re-adorning and re-dressing — I cannot call these renewing in the true inward sense.

The Counter-Reformation blew air into an old balloon. Rubens and the reconquest for the Roman Church of Poland, Hungary, and Czechoslovakia, the Jesuits in South America and the French on Lake Champlain, the Council of Trent and the sculptures of Bernini — I cannot see them as Christianity in *essence*. I see them as ecclesiology in quintessence, but not Christianity in essence.

Take the case of the old Anglo-Catholics in the Church of England, who referred to their movement as "church revival" versus the "evangelical revival" of Whitefield and Wesley. If the Anglo-Catholics were referring to the redesignation of the Eucharist as holy and urgent food and drink for needy people, then I am with them, at least in aspiration. If they were talking about religion and not form, then I am with them. If, on the other hand, Catholic Anglicans had in mind Sir Gilbert Scott and the renewal of church edifices, the "beauty of holiness" and the principle of "reserve in religion," then I cannot stand with them. Renewal movements have to be instances of soteriology or they are not part of Christ's centrifugal influence on human tragedy and human exhaustedness the world over.

Soteriology trumps sociology. It trumps worship. It trumps beauty. It trumps patriotism. It even trumps historicism, although it has to be anchored in history.

Soteriology trumps friendship. It trumps — this is a big statement — erotic and romantic love. It trumps gender. It trumps race. It even trumps parents and children. This is because it extends the search of God to the abysses and holocausts of human dereliction, the extremes of experience and suffering.

Why did nineteenth-century people respond to Danish sculptor Bertil Thorwaldsen's statue of the *Compassionate Christ* in the contagious way they did? The statue, which evoked the welcoming Jesus of Nazareth, wounded hands stretched out in greeting and embrace, was copied everywhere. Copies of the statue could not be created fast enough. They are still in churches from Potsdam, Germany, to Birmingham, Alabama. The statue caught something: the compassion of the Man for Others as described in the Gospels.

The same could be said of Warner Sallman's "kitschy" painting of the head of Christ (1924). A coffee-table book has been written about this picture,[8] a respectful book, which collects hundreds of letters from everyday Americans who have stated what the picture means to them. I respond to the painting myself. To me, it conveys the resolution, the human transparency, the divine light, the love of the man. For me the picture is in a straight line with the centrifugal force of the historical Jesus. When I look at it, I feel connected to the First Christian.

It was touching, to me almost supremely touching, that the *New York Times* photograph in April 2002 of the first little funeral procession for Pakistani Christian women and children killed in a terrorist raid on a crowded chapel captured this arresting image: one of the men in the ragged cluster of people was holding up a picture of Sallman's *Jesus*. It was the universal note in an otherwise contextualized atrocity in the aftermath of September 11, 2001. A man was holding up Sallman's *Jesus*. For him, that was what there was to say.

It may be that in another time, in a future period of history, Christianity will need to recover again a contextualized Jesus. We may need once again to be delivered from a docetic universal man. We may need to pull away from an Alexandrian Christ, the divine cosmic redeemer, to an Antiochene one, a human struggler within and also against the overwhelming, constraining influences of context.

But that is not our problem now! Our problem now, which mirrors the world's, is that we need to travel once more toward the universal characteristics of religion. These are themes such as humility and repentance; God's victory, not ours; the depth of meaning behind all actions, where motive is the key thing; the particular meaning in all human intentions that is narcissistic, libidinal, and violently angry; and the exclusive focus in Jesus on the lost and the bad rather than on the good and the great.

8. *Icons of American Protestantism: The Art of Warner Sallman*, ed. David Morgan (New Haven: Yale University Press, 1996).

Jesus was the First Christian, whose discontinuities were the seed of his universal interest and aptness. This was because of his astonishing will to say one thing: Repent, everyone, for you cannot save your fargone selves. I have come for you as if you in your miredness were the only person in the world.

A Meditation at Christmas

In some ways, Christmas decontextualizes the historical Jesus more than any other time. We do not know at what time of the year he was born. There was almost definitely no snow on the ground in Judea. And there is no proof, beyond strong and early tradition, that Christ was born at Bethlehem. Even David Flusser, normally so reverent in his handling of the Gospels, thinks Christ was born at Nazareth.

Yet I cannot give up on Christmas. Far from it, for Christmas captures basic elements in the centrifugal force of Jesus of Nazareth. It has for many hundreds of years carried, inside the long train of its tradition, signals of Christ "as he really was." Christmas bears the saving theme, the theme of human lostness, the theme of the smallest seed growing to stature, the centrifugal "magnitude of weakness" (Christopher Smart).

The continuity of every time with the discontinuous Christ of that particular time is expressed undyingly through two nineteenth-century American Christmas carols. These are still sung and heard today, from ice-skating rinks in Tokyo to almost all Christian churches in English-speaking countries to airports worldwide in December to shopping malls and Cracker Barrel restaurants. They are Phillips Brooks's 1867 hymn "O little town of Bethlehem" and Edmund Hamilton Sears's 1846 hymn "It came upon the midnight clear." Each of these carols is a pure example of the living centrifugal force of the historical Jesus.

Phillips Brooks wrote his hymn for a children's play in Holy Trinity Church, Rittenhouse Square, Philadelphia. He envisaged the contextualized Bethlehem, a town that he had in fact recently visited, in decontextualized terms: "The hopes and fears of all the years are met in thee tonight." In theology, this is called "salvation history," a phrase coined by the Germans.

It means that Bethlehem has significance beyond its particular existence. Its historical existence is given, by virtue of Christ's birth, universal existence and significance. Christianity holds the concrete and the general here in perfect tension. Bethlehem is a town like no other. At the same time it is a town like all others, in which all other towns exist representatively.

In the third stanza of his hymn, Brooks, who was a liberal evangelical,[1] carries forward the main centrifugal idea of Jesus' historical ministry:

No ear may hear his coming, But in this world of sin,
Where meek souls will receive him still, The dear Christ enters in.

The world consists of sin. The two are almost synonymous. Jesus' damning anthropology is in force. It is at work in the idea. Brooks, despite his generally optimistic worldview, cannot deny the fact. Yet, too, the humbling repentance of the one to whom Jesus addresses his Word is evoked. It is the "meek souls" who receive him. It is not the "righteous" and "those who have no need of a physician." The Physician, the

---

1. The term is a proper noun and has a precise meaning. It means that Brooks identified with the Evangelical or "low-church" party within the American Episcopal church of the time. But he was on the left wing of the Evangelical Party. He was a "liberal" in his understanding of the Bible and biblical criticism and a "liberal" in his desire to learn from the world's insights, especially from science. He and his students and associates in the Episcopal Church became known as the "liberal Evangelicals." Within fifty years, the "Evangelical" part of the movement dropped away: but the term "liberal" (enhanced now by "broad-church") stayed.

See Gillis J. Harp's "'We Cannot Spare You': Phillips Brooks' Break with the Evangelical Party, 1859-1873," in *Church History* 68, no. 4 (1999): 930-53.

"dear Christ," comes to those who require his services. Repentance equals meekness. The world equals sin. The "dear Christ" is the Man Between, the One who is still "here" in force, because the second Son of Man has not yet come. The gospel of the historical Jesus is entirely, concentratedly represented here.

The hymn concludes with a prayer, the poet's response to the time- and place-breaking statement of universality springing from context:

> O holy Child of Bethlehem! Descend to us, we pray;
> Cast out our sin and enter in, Be born in us today.

Context, be universalized right now! We are like the old ones who needed a physician, who needed an exorcist: "Cast out our sin." Save us to the extent of rebirthing us body and soul.

This is a recognition of original sin and a statement of the human problem to the furthest degree. We must be born again. Phillips Brooks's evangelicalism is in perfect harmony with the One who he believed had called him. The hymn is a classic case of the First Christian's extended universal reach.

Edmund Hamilton Sears was a clergyman affected by the Unitarian controversy in New England, which so influenced American "high culture" before the Civil War. Sears wrote several hymns, but his most familiar one is a second, almost perfect example of the centrifugal force deriving from Jesus the Christian.

> It came upon the midnight clear,
> That glorious song of old,
> From angels bending near the earth
> To touch their harps of gold:
> "Peace on the earth, good will to men,
> From heav'n's all-gracious King."
> The world in solemn stillness lay
> To hear the angels sing.

Still through the cloven skies they come,
With peaceful wings unfurled,
And still their heav'nly music floats
O'er all the weary world;
Above its sad and lowly plains
They bend on hov'ring wing,
And ever o'er its Babel-sounds
The blessed angels sing.

The context is "of old," yet "Still . . . they come"! The world is a
tainted, troubled, guilty place: "its sad and lowly plains." Yet "ever o'er
its Babel-sounds, the blessed angels sing."

Sears's anthropology is Christ's, but the stage is Maine, 1846:

Yet with the woes of sin and strife The world has suffered long;
Beneath in heav'nly strain have rolled Two thousand years of wrong.

Sears was an early "Social Gospel" man. He discerned the social or so-
ciological factor in the (collective) heart that Jesus had described in the
words concerning "purity control." Sears's context was "early New England liberal"; Jesus' was what it was. The two mesh perfectly because
of the universalizing energy of Christ's centrifugal force.

At the same time, Sears knew the personal, individual side of the
anthropology. Mankind is burdened and oppressed; the individual is
burdened and oppressed. Original sin is social, but it is also personal.

O ye, beneath life's crushing load, Whose forms are bending low,
Who toil along the climbing way With painful steps and slow, . . .
Look now! For glad and golden hours Come swiftly on the wing;
O rest beside the weary road And hear the angels sing!

This stanza, the fourth, is omitted in most hymnals today. It is considered individualistic. I don't know. I *do* know that it was in the 1940
Episcopal hymnal but was dropped from the 1982 edition. I do know
that it is not to be found in most collections of Christmas carols.

Sears's anthropology is clear. The oppressed, lamed, bent man is the one who hears.

> For lo! the days are hast'ning on, By prophets seen of old,
> When with the ever-circling years Shall come the time foretold,
> When peace shall over all the earth Its ancient splendors fling,
> And the whole world give back the song Which now the angels sing.

Sears's last verse enters into the "open-ended" atmosphere of Christ's eschatology. One day, the "Peace on earth" spoken once at Bethlehem, the "salvation-historical" greeting that made Bethlehem a representative context, will address the whole world in implementation rather than hope. Then "shall come the time foretold."

We live in the second chapter of a three-part plan. We are deep in the second, stuck in the middle of it. There is time to hear, time to agree, time to give up, time to accept the Christ's diagnosis of total depravity, time to reckon ourselves among the tax collectors and sinners, time to resign from the company of all who have no need of a physician, time to join the sinners, the impious whom Christ justified by his intent and first presence.

Christmas is always the First Time, in Bethlehem of Judea, and always also the Last Time, maybe. "For lo! the days are hast'ning on." The universality of the Jesus context, broken and stretched and pulled out further to reach newly appearing contexts, will at one point of time become a single context. In retrospect, the universal context of the Christ at Bethlehem will be changed into the Christ of a single period of history, the period that lasted from his coming at the time of John to his final coming in the time of the Son of Man. After that, there will be no new contexts to inform. All contexts will disappear forever, as at the end of the *Divine Comedy*. They will all be swallowed up and outshone by a single blinding lamp that is the Son of God.

Selected Reading List

Atkinson, James. *Christianity and Judaism: New Understanding, New Relationship.* Oxford: Latimer House, 1984.

Baeck, Leo. "Romantic Religion." In *Judaism and Christianity.* Essays translated with an introduction by Walter Kaufmann. Pp. 189-291. Philadelphia: Jewish Publication Society of America, 1958.

Bornkamm, Heinrich. *Luther and the Old Testament.* Philadelphia: Fortress Press, 1969.

Bultmann, Rudolf. *Primitive Christianity in Its Contemporary Setting.* Trans. R. H. Fuller. New York: Meridian Books, 1957.

Dodds, E. R. *Pagan and Christian in an Age of Anxiety.* Cambridge: Cambridge University Press, 1965.

Dunn, J. D. G. *The Partings of the Ways Between Christianity and Judaism and Their Significance for the Character of Christianity.* London: SCM, 1991.

Flusser, David. *Jesus.* 3rd edition. Jerusalem: The Magnes Press, 2001.

Frymer-Kensky, Tikva; David Novak, Peter Ochs, David Fox Sandmel, and Michael A. Signer, editors. *Christianity in Jewish Terms.* Boulder: Westview Press, 2000.

Fuller, Reginald. "Justification in Recent Pauline Studies." *Anglican Theological Review* 84, no. 2 (Spring 2002): 411-16.

Funk, Robert. "The Jesus Seminar and the Quest." In *Jesus Then and Now: Images of Jesus in History and Christology,* edited by Marvin Meyer and Charles Hughes. Harrisburg, Pa.: Trinity Press International, 2001.

Gehring, Roger. *Hausgemeinde und Mission. Die Bedeutung antiker Häuser und Hausgemeinschaften von Jesus bis Paulus.* Brunnen: TVG, 2000.

Hagner, Donald A. *The Jewish Reclamation of Jesus: An Analysis and Critique of Modern Jewish Study of Jesus.* Grand Rapids: Zondervan, 1984.

Harrington, Daniel J. "Retrieving the Jewishness of Jesus: Recent Developments." In *The Historical Jesus Through Catholic and Jewish Eyes,* edited by Leonard J. Greenspoon, Dennis Hamm, S.J., and Bryan F. LeBeau. Harrisburg, Pa.: Trinity Press International, 2000.

Helsted, Dyveke; Eva Henschen, and Bjarne Jørnaes. *Thorwaldsen.* Copenhagen: The Thorwaldsen Museum, 1990.

Hengel, Martin, and C. K. Barrett. *Conflicts and Challenges in Early Christianity.* Edited by Donald A. Hagner. Harrisburg, Pa.: Trinity Press International, 1999.

Käsemann, Ernst. *Essays on New Testament Themes.* Philadelphia: Fortress Press, 1982.

————. *New Testament Questions of Today.* London: SCM, 1969.

————. *Jesus Means Freedom.* Philadelphia: Fortress Press, 1968.

Klenicki, Rabbi Leon, editor. *Toward a Theological Encounter: Jewish Understandings of Christianity.* Mahwah, N.J.: Paulist Press, 1991.

Moltmann, Jürgen. *Jesus Christ for Today's World.* Minneapolis: Fortress Press, 1994.

Morgan, David, editor. *Icons of American Protestantism: The Art of Warner Sallman.* New Haven and London: Yale University Press, 1996.

Neill, Stephen, with N. T. Wright. *The Interpretation of the New Testament, 1861-1986.* Oxford and New York: Oxford University Press, 1988.

Riches, John. *A Century of New Testament Study.* Cambridge: Lutterworth Press, 1993.

Sanders, E. P. *Paul and Palestinian Judaism: A Comparison of Patterns of Religion.* Philadelphia: Fortress Press, 1977.

Schweitzer, Albert. *The Quest of the Historical Jesus: A Critical Study of Its Progress from Reimarus to Wrede.* New York: Macmillan, 1968.

Steiner, George. *No Passion Spent: Essays 1978-1995.* New Haven and London: Yale University Press, 1996.

Stuhlmacher, Peter. *Biblische Theologie des Neuen Testaments.* Band I. Grundlegung von Jesus zu Paulus. Göttingen: Vandenhoeck & Ruprecht, 1992.

Vermes, Geza. *The Religion of Jesus the Jew.* Minneapolis: Fortress Press, 1997.

Wilson, Marvin. *Our Father Abraham: Jewish Roots of the Christian Faith.* Grand Rapids: Eerdmans, 1989.

Wright, N. T. *Jesus and the Victory of God.* Minneapolis: Fortress Press, 1990.

Zahl, Paul F. M. *Die Rechtfertigungslehre Ernst Käsemanns.* Stuttgart: Calwer Verlag, 1996.

Index of Authors

Index of Biblical References